W9-BYK-377

THIS JOURNAL
BELONGS TO:

Liv

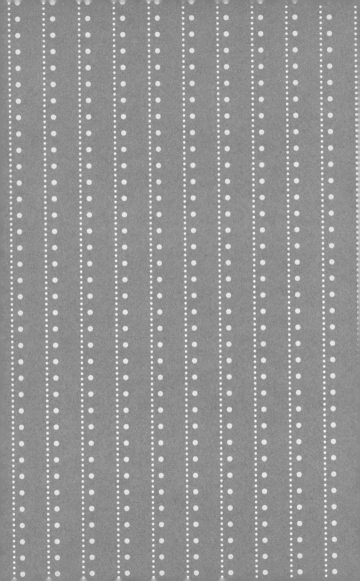

THE
POSITIVE
JOURNAL

Nancy F. Clark

5 Minutes
a Day
Toward a
Happier
Life

STERLING
New York

STERLING
New York

An Imprint of Sterling Publishing Co., Inc.
1166 Avenue of the Americas
New York, NY 10036

ISBN 978-1-4549-2502-6

Distributed in Canada by Sterling Publishing Co., Inc.
c/o Canadian Manda Group, 664 Annette Street
Toronto, Ontario M6S 2C8, Canada
Distributed in the United Kingdom by GMC Distribution Services
Castle Place, 166 High Street, Lewes, East Sussex BN7 1XU, England
Distributed in Australia by NewSouth Books
University of New South Wales, Sydney, NSW 2052, Australia

For information about custom editions, special sales, and premium
and corporate purchases, please contact Sterling Special Sales
at 800-805-5489 or specialsales@sterlingpublishing.com.

Manufactured in China

4 6 8 10 9 7 5

sterlingpublishing.com

Cover design by Elizabeth Lindy
Interior design by Barbara Balch

Cover art by Vaju Ariel/Shutterstock

INTRODUCTION

The Positive Journal is designed to give you science-backed nuggets of information about positive psychology, gratitude, confidence, communication, meaning, and purpose. It also includes a variety of other topics that will help develop a happier and more fulfilling life—for you. All you have to do is decide that this is what you want and that it's worth five minutes a day. You can start today. It's as easy as that!

Daily mini lessons are presented to you in a precise order that will guide you to build a happier and more rewarding life in a manner that is backed by research. If you spend five minutes a day reflecting and writing, you'll be noticeably happier in the first week.

Much of the information is surprisingly counterintuitive. Many would think that writing about gratitude every day would be better than once a week. But research shows that's not quite accurate. This is why I'll be guiding you to write about gratitude one day a week.

JOURNALING BENEFIT MESSAGE

To truly learn from a self-help book, you need to interact with the information. One way you can do that is to write answers to your daily exercises right here in this journal.

● ● ●

Want to Be Happier? You probably realize that everybody has a different happiness level. Do you think that genetics or life situations determine those levels? Well yes, partially. Do you think it's 90 percent or 95 percent? Nope. Only 60 percent of your happiness is determined by your genetics and circumstances. So, you've got a full 40 percent under your control. Isn't that great? I'll be showing you how to work with that 40 percent so you can become a much happier person. The first thing you must do is make the decision to become happier.

Today Write about your decision to work on this 40 percent of happiness, which is under your control. Is it worth five minutes a day to you? Cheers in advance for you!

It's worth the 5 minutes,
I'm so sick of feeling
unhappy when I have so much
to be grateful for. It slips
my mind sometimes. I wish I
felt it more mentally but the
physicality of it all breaks
me down mentally. I don't know
what to do, I'm stuck.

● ● ●

Write or Wrong? Now you might think the more gratitude journaling you do, the better your life will become. Well, I'm sorry to say that would be wrong. I've consulted with positivity psychologists, research scientists, and expert life coaches to bring you their latest advice throughout this book. Studies by professor and author Sonja Lyubomirsky found that people who journaled about gratitude once or twice a week were happier than those who did it daily. I'll be guiding you to do this once a week.

Today Gratitude can be for big things or little things. Since we're just starting out, write about three big things that make you feel grateful.

My Family ⎱
              ⎰ Support
My Friends ⎱

My past for making me
who I am and teaching
me lessons

• • •

Advice from Emma Stanford science director and author of *The Happiness Track* Emma Seppälä, says using self-criticism liberally is a success myth. Self-criticism is not the key to self-improvement. Self-compassion is the key, which allows you to be successful without sabotaging yourself. When you fail, you should talk to yourself kindly and say something like, "Everyone makes mistakes now and then. At least I'm trying." Or maybe, "Failure is not the opposite of success, it's part of success."

Today Write about what you'll say to yourself the next time you make a mistake.

"Everyone makes mistakes, don't dwell on it. Everything turns out how its supposed to."

• • •

Glimmer of Hope Professor Barbara Fredrickson, author of *Positivity*, says that negative emotions hit us like a sledgehammer. They're more intense than our positive emotions because we have an ingrained negativity bias. Telling someone, "Be happy" or "Forget about it" is not appropriate for many of the ups and downs in life. However, even when something bad happens, a glimmer of hope plays a role in helping a person make the upward climb back toward happiness.

Today Think of something negative that happened to you that had a glimmer of hope. Write about what happened and what kept you going.

Ciera and I broke up because I needed to focus on myself. I miss her but my hope is that I will not just get better mentally but physically too. ♡

• • •

Reset My Emotions Please Professor Fredrickson's research shows that positive emotions actually act as a reset button on your negative emotions. Sharing positive emotions with multiple people is more gratifying than if we experience it alone.

Today Write about something positive that has happened to you that you could share with more than one person. By doing this, each of you will be raising your own positivity levels. That's pretty great, isn't it?

_____

_____

_____

_____

_____

_____

_____

_____

_____

• • •

Start Rewriting Your New Story Who says you have to stick with your life as it is? Instead of giving your attention to "what I don't want," focus on "what I want." Picture it clearly and give it your full attention, just as Olympic athletes are trained to do.

Today Write about your new story, your "what I want" story.

_____

_____

_____

_____

_____

_____

_____

_____

_____

_____

_____

_____

● ● ●

What Day Is Your Kindness Day? Research by Professor Lyubomirsky has shown that focusing on kindness one day a week is ideal. Of course you should be kind every day, but focusing on doing three acts of kindness once a week is more beneficial. This can be as simple as smiling at a stranger or opening the door for someone, or as big as introducing people to others who can help them.

Today Write about one kind act you could do next week to help someone. Merely anticipating the action has a hidden benefit for you: it delivers a happy-brain chemical, which we'll be discussing later on.

_____

_____

_____

_____

_____

_____

_____

_____

● ● ●

Include Unfun, Too Dr. Timothy Sharp, Chief Happiness Officer of the Happiness Institute in Australia, says that in addition to pleasure and enjoyment, satisfaction is also an important part of happiness. When you're planning your tasks, include things that might not be fun but will give you a sense of achievement.

Today What tasks or activities do you have planned that will give you a satisfying sense of achievement?

_____

_____

_____

_____

_____

_____

_____

_____

_____

_____

• • •

Savor Together Fred Bryant, social psychologist and coauthor of *Savoring*, says that we don't often make the most of good things that happen to us. When we relish good moments with others, it strengthens those bonds and prolongs relationships. Think of inviting someone out to lunch or dinner and telling them that the purpose is for both of you to savor everything.

Today Who is this person, and where would you like to go?

_____

_____

_____

_____

_____

_____

_____

_____

_____

_____

_____

● ● ●

Relationship Muscles Think about someone you would like to have a stronger relationship with. Decide you will savor with them something good that has happened to you recently and savor something they're grateful for as well. This will be a boost for both of you and your relationship.

Today Write about the person you've chosen and how this will make you feel.

_____

_____

_____

_____

_____

_____

_____

_____

_____

_____

● ● ●

Positive or Negative? A savoring study was done by dividing people into two groups. One group was asked to take a 20-minute walk and look for positive things to savor. The other group was asked to look for negative things. After doing this every day for one week, the positive group reported feeling much happier than the negative group.

Today News reporting gets more attention from communicating negative situations. I want you to begin searching for positive reports. Write about a positive piece of news you've heard recently. Did this make you feel happier?

_____

_____

_____

_____

_____

_____

_____

_____

_____

• • •

Savor with a Mental Photograph Take a mental photograph of a friend's laugh or a scene outside your window. Right now, look around you for three positive things. Think about how this moment of savoring makes you feel grateful.

Gratitude Day Write about three big blessings in your life that make you feel grateful.

_____

_____

_____

_____

_____

_____

_____

_____

_____

_____

● ● ●

Sharpen Your Senses Clinical psychologist Erica Chadwick suggests slowing down during meals. It's important to take the time to focus on just one of your senses. Smell the food, or close your eyes while taking a sip of a drink.

(Reminder: tomorrow is Kindness Day.)

Today What item of food or drink did you thoroughly enjoy recently?

_____

_____

_____

_____

_____

_____

_____

_____

_____

_____

_____

● ● ●

Give and Give a Little More Adam Grant, professor at Wharton Business School and author of _Give and Take_ and _Originals_, advises you to focus a little more attention on giving to others without expecting anything in return. This can be done at work, with friends, or at home.

Today Write about how you could give a gift of your time or connections to someone without expecting anything in return.

_____

_____

_____

_____

_____

_____

_____

❏ **Kindness Day** Did you do three acts of kindness in the last 24 hours? If you're especially proud of one, add it to your Kindness Treasures page at the end of this journal.

● ● ●

Is This One? One thing we know is that experiencing authentic positive emotions is healthy and promotes a host of benefits, such as broadening awareness, building new resources, and making social connections. Professor Fredrickson advises you to develop an eye for the positive happening throughout your day by asking, "Is this one of those positive things?"

Today Write about something that may come up tomorrow and offer you an opportunity to ask yourself that question.

_____

_____

_____

_____

_____

_____

_____

_____

_____

_____

• • •

First Question Life coach Caren Osten says when she picks up her tenth-grade son from school, she asks him to tell her something good that happened during his day. Of course, he rolls his eyes at first but then comes up with something he's happy about. This puts a positive spin on the conversation.

Today What's something positive that happened to you this past week? (You didn't roll your eyes at me, did you?)

_____

_____

_____

_____

_____

_____

_____

_____

_____

• • •

Happiness Boost Researchers found that the following exercise created an immediate boost in happiness.

> *Imagine yourself in the future. Everything has gone as well as it possibly could. You've worked hard and succeeded in accomplishing all of your life goals. You're living the life of your dreams. You're now identifying the best possible way things might turn out in your life.*

Today Take a few minutes to write about what you saw and how you felt. Do you think this might help guide your decisions now?

_____

_____

_____

_____

_____

_____

_____

_____

_____

• • •

Be a Game Changer Tech entrepreneur Mary Spio, who grew up in Ghana, has succeeded against difficult circumstances. In answer to how she became such a great game changer, she says that some people think, "If a situation or event doesn't affect me, why should I bother? I have my own problems to contend with." When we ignore things, we miss the opportunity for positive change. We have the chance to truly get to know each other in our connected world and search for solutions to help each other in our journey to joy.

Today Write about a time when you got involved and helped solve a problem.

_____

_____

_____

_____

_____

_____

_____

_____

_____

• • •

Top Ten Psychologists used to focus on negative emotions such as anger, fear, or sadness. Now there's a field of positive psychology. It has been discovered that focusing on positive emotions can strongly influence our level of happiness. The top ten positive emotions are (drumroll please): *joy, gratitude, serenity, interest, hope, pride, amusement, inspiration, awe,* and *love.* We'll deal with these one at a time because I told you this is a five-minute-a-day journal. Today's topic—the first on our list—is *joy.* Joy is the feeling you get during a perfect moment in time, such as a beautiful holiday dinner or when seeing your child succeed.

Gratitude Day Write about one moment of joy that quickly comes to mind and include how grateful you are to have experienced it.

_____

_____

_____

_____

_____

_____

_____

_____

• • •

Pay It Forward The second positive emotion is *gratitude*. Gratitude is when you're greatly moved by a situation, or when you realize someone has gone out of their way to do something for you. You'll often feel that you want to pay it forward. I believe these "pay it forward" desires make the world a better place.

(Reminder: tomorrow is Kindness Day.)

Bonus Gratitude Day List three small things that make you grateful.

_____

_____

_____

_____

_____

_____

_____

_____

_____

• • •

Softness or Serenity The third positive emotion is *serenity*. Serenity is what you feel on a peaceful day. It's when you realize there's nothing more you have to do and surrender yourself to the moment. It's also when you're enjoying a favorite luxury and savoring it completely.

Today Think about a time you experienced serenity. Wouldn't you love to add another one to your calendar? Maybe a massage?

_____

_____

_____

_____

_____

_____

_____

_____

_____

❑ **Kindness Day** Did you do three acts of kindness in the last 24 hours? If not, what type of a reminder would be best for you? A sticky note, or perhaps a phone reminder?

● ● ●

Something New The fourth positive emotion is *interest*. Interest is an awakened state that calls your attention to something new and arouses your curiosity and fascination. It invigorates you.

Today Write about one thing that interests you and leaves you wanting more.

_____

_____

_____

_____

_____

_____

_____

_____

_____

_____

_____

_____

• • •

Possibility of Hope The fifth positive emotion is *hope*. Professor Fredrickson says that we feel hope when things take a turn for the worse. When we have hope, it opens up the possibility that things can change and get better.

Today Write about a difficult situation where you had a strong sense of hope. Do you feel that hope helped you get through it?

_____

_____

_____

_____

_____

_____

_____

_____

_____

_____

_____

• • •

Pat Your Back The sixth positive emotion is *pride*. When you stretch yourself and attain something you thought might be impossible, you experience pride and deserve to pat yourself on the back. Now, how could anything be wrong with that? When coupled with humility and modesty, pride is a positive feeling.

Today Write about a time when you deservedly felt pride.

_____

_____

_____

_____

_____

_____

_____

_____

_____

_____

_____

• • •

Makes You Laugh The seventh positive emotion is _amusement_. Amusement can be thought of as those delightful surprises that make you laugh—those unexpected moments that interrupt your focus and crack you up. Within a moment, it can shatter boredom and change your perspective.

Today What has been amusing for you recently? Doesn't merely thinking about it make you happier?

_____

_____

_____

_____

_____

_____

_____

_____

_____

_____

_____

● ● ●

Seek Inspiration The eighth positive emotion is *inspiration*. Inspiration is something that touches your spirit. As Professor Fredrickson says, inspiration happens when you witness an unlikely triumph, when you're watching the sunset, or when reading something profound. I love how a quotation, a beautiful photo, or an exquisite piece of art can instantly inspire me.

Gratitude Day Write about three inspiring things you've seen or experienced.

_____

_____

_____

_____

_____

_____

_____

_____

_____

_____

● ● ●

What Are Your Awe Triggers? The ninth positive emotion is *awe*. Awe is the feeling you get when something fills you with wonder and amazement. Awe is triggered when we are faced with the endless bounty of nature or the universe.

(Reminder: tomorrow is Kindness Day.)

Today Write about a time when you experienced awe. If you're so inclined, how about a tiny sketch?

_____

_____

_____

_____

_____

_____

_____

_____

_____

_____

_____

● ● ●

The Love Experience The tenth positive emotion is *love*. Professor Fredrickson describes love as encompassing all of the positive emotions listed in the preceding pages. Love is all that and more. When we experience love, our bodies are flooded with feel-good hormones that reduce stress and even lengthen our lives.

Today Write about a time when you experienced love.

_____

_____

_____

_____

_____

_____

_____

_____

_____

❏ **Kindness Day** Did you do three acts of kindness in the last 24 hours?

• • •

Time Is Valuable Charles Duhigg, author of *Smarter Faster Better*, says the most productive people don't have more time. They are just better at motivating themselves to think more intently about what actually matters instead of reacting to the demands around them.

Today Write about something that's not important but is taking up your valuable time.

_____

_____

_____

_____

_____

_____

_____

_____

_____

_____

• • •

Contemplate This Take Charles Duhigg's advice and copy the most productive people by setting up contemplative routines in your life. These can be habits you turn to that allow you to reflect on your actions and decisions. Journaling is a great habit, because it creates a space for contemplation.

Today Write about something that's very important for you to spend time on. The most important thing is to write about why this is significant.

_____

_____

_____

_____

_____

_____

_____

_____

_____

_____

_____

• • •

Why Oh Why? Thinking about why something is important allows you to become more productive, more creative, and happier. You're not happier because you turn your brain off. Instead, you're happier because you are thinking more deeply about what actually matters.

Today Since it's lucky that you're journaling now, write about how journaling will help you become more productive.

_____

_____

_____

_____

_____

_____

_____

_____

_____

_____

● ● ●

Date _____   Week 5 • Day 4

Brain Happy Getting to make choices makes your brain happy!
Add to its happiness by looking for opportunities to take control, make a choice, or by expressing your unique style. It can
be something as simple as deciding whether to have Indian or
Italian food for lunch.

Today Write about a situation that may come up in the next
24 hours where you'll get to make a choice. Make the decision now and you'll get double the benefit. Your brain will be
choice-happy, and you'll be able to look forward to something,
activating the anticipating-a-reward part of your brain.

_____

_____

_____

_____

_____

_____

_____

_____

_____

• • •

Don't Settle for Less Don't let fear make you settle in life. There may be many things you want, but far more significant are the things you need that allow you to live an authentic life. Caroline Myss, author of *Anatomy of the Spirit*, says that when you begin putting your needs before your wants, you're becoming more in tune with your inner life.

Gratitude Day Write about an important choice you made that may have had challenges but brought you a gratifying and fulfilling experience. This is an important Gratitude Day entry!

_____

_____

_____

_____

_____

_____

_____

_____

_____

_____

• • •

Slack Off! Christine Carter, author of *The Sweet Spot*, recommends that you slack off strategically. She slacks off for 10 minutes a day walking through a park near her office. She then slacks off for another 20 minutes at the end of the day by reading in her daughter's room while she's doing her homework. She says she's found that slacking off makes her more productive because she slacks strategically, meaning she takes breaks at specific times; this improves her focus when she gets back to work.

(Reminder: tomorrow is Kindness Day.)

Today Where and when do you plan to slack off?

_____

_____

_____

_____

_____

_____

_____

_____

● ● ●

Money for Kindness In a study, people were separated into two groups, and each person was given the same amount of money. One group was told to spend it on themselves, and the other group was told to spend it on someone else. Those who spent the money on others reported feeling happier. We'll look into this further in future weeks.

Today Write about one time you spent money on someone else. How did you feel?

_____

_____

_____

_____

_____

_____

_____

_____

❑ **Kindness Day** Did you do three acts of kindness in the last 24 hours?

● ● ●

Top of Your List Put happiness at the top of your list of priorities. If you don't, other things will get in the way of your happiness.

Today Write your priority list for the next 24 hours.

_____

_____

_____

_____

_____

_____

_____

_____

_____

_____

_____

_____

_____

_____

• • •

Set a Happy Goal The successful pursuit of happiness requires planning with goals. Make sure your goals are SMART (specific, measurable, achievable, relevant, and timed).

Today What's one happiness goal that's SMART?

_____

_____

_____

_____

_____

_____

_____

_____

_____

_____

_____

_____

_____

● ● ●

Happy Breaks Do little things that make you happy. In the middle of a stressful day, take a break and do something that makes you happy for a brief moment.

Today Write about something you could do in just a few minutes that would give you a happy break.

_____

_____

_____

_____

_____

_____

_____

_____

_____

_____

_____

_____

● ● ●

Share the Good Stacey Kennelly from the Greater Good Science Center says there's plenty of advice for coping with life's negative events, but what about dealing with the good events?

Today One way to expand on your goodness is to share it with someone else. Name one person you've shared something good with recently, and describe how this made you feel.

_____

_____

_____

_____

_____

_____

_____

_____

_____

_____

● ● ●

Create Your Happy List Be on the lookout for new ways to be happy. Decide where you'll keep your list and remember that you want to have fun.

Gratitude Day Write about three ways you've been happy in the past. See, you've started your list. Do you feel that grateful feeling?

_____

_____

_____

_____

_____

_____

_____

_____

_____

_____

• • •

Stress to Succeed? In the last year, have you felt stressed, exhausted, or burnt out? You may have been pushing yourself at work or at home, because this is what most people think they need to do to succeed. Stanford science director Emma Seppälä says that drive is a positive thing, but only in doses. The problem is that we're living in overdrive. Research and our own personal experiences are showing that we're paying a high price for it with chronic stress.

(Reminder: tomorrow is Kindness Day.)

Today Write about a stressful situation that happened in the past. To keep you from falling into a negative mood, write about how you could handle it better today.

_____

_____

_____

_____

_____

_____

_____

_____

● ● ●

Tiny Kindness Start small when you're beginning a kindness and generosity habit. Think of your current connections and identify who may need your help.

Today Write about how you can help someone you know.

_____

_____

_____

_____

_____

_____

_____

_____

_____

_____

_____

❑ **Kindness Day** Did you do three acts of kindness in the last 24 hours?

• • •

Face a Limiting Fear If you have an unnecessary fear that's limiting your life, here's what you can do. Positive psychology expert and coach Homaira Kabir says that the next time you feel fear in your mind or body, identify what you are avoiding. Try to understand the inner voice that's feeling low. Tell yourself that you are capable, you are important, and that you are able to accomplish anything. Now, with this newfound strength, face the fears that are holding you back!

Today Write about a fear that you're proud of overcoming in the past.

_____

_____

_____

_____

_____

_____

_____

_____

_____

• • •

Other-Worth Try to curb yourself from seeking approval and validation from others. You can't control how other people think of and view you. Instead, do things for your own approval. Self-help author Wayne Dyer said that you cannot rely on others to deem you worthy. You're important because you say so. Depending on others to give you value is considered to be "other-worth."

Today Write about an area of your life where you need to curb seeking approval from others. Also, write about the positive things you'll say to yourself for doing a good job!

_____

_____

_____

_____

_____

_____

_____

_____

_____

• • •

Increase Your Positives Relationship researcher and psychologist John Gottman specializes in love psychology. He's found that you must have five positive interactions for every negative interaction, because negative emotions such as contempt and defensiveness have more power to hurt a relationship.

Today I'm not going to guide you today. I'm going to let you choose something positive to write about.

_____

_____

_____

_____

_____

_____

_____

_____

_____

_____

_____

• • •

Me, Meditate? Mediation has been shown to greatly increase happiness and positivity while decreasing stress. Many years ago, I decided to get up 15 minutes earlier and give it a try. Now it's something I can't go without. I like to listen to time-guided meditations so I won't have to worry about running off schedule. Has meditation been beneficial for you? Do you believe it would be helpful for you to work into your schedule?

Today Write about your general stress level and if you think meditation or even mindful moments are, or should be, important to you.

_____

_____

_____

_____

_____

_____

_____

_____

_____

• • •

Deep Diving Gratitude journaling in detail is especially satisfying.

Gratitude Day Today write in depth about a particular thing that makes you grateful. Pretend you're writing a minimovie using all of your senses.

_____

_____

_____

_____

_____

_____

_____

_____

_____

_____

_____

• • •

Releasing Judgment In the next 24 hours, I would like to surprise you. Look around at strangers—maybe someone standing next to you in a line. Pick a person who looks the opposite of who you think you would like. Smile at them, make a comment, or ask them a question. Honestly, every time I've done this, I've been pleasantly surprised, and you will be, too. Our judgments are blinders to a full life.

(Reminder: tomorrow is Kindness Day.)

Today Write about the types of people you don't think you would like. Go ahead and admit your judgments. It's good for you. Now add one person who meets any of these descriptions who you've found you liked.

_____

_____

_____

_____

_____

_____

_____

_____

• • •

Use Your Senses As we discussed earlier this week, journaling in detail using all of your senses is important.

Today I'd like you to write about a kind thing someone did for you, like cooking you a delicious meal. Write about this in detail, including how it made you feel.

_____

_____

_____

_____

_____

_____

_____

_____

_____

❏ **Kindness Day** Did you do three acts of kindness in the last 24 hours? This is helping you on your way to living a happier, more fulfilling life.

● ● ●

Following Your Passion? If you aren't following your passion, I advise you to think about changing your story to own your uniqueness. Visualize three circles: one is what you're passionate about, one is where your talents lie, and one is what supports your life in time or money. Living at the intersection of these three means having a more fulfilling life.

Today Draw three circles and fill in the first thoughts that occur to you. Let your intuition guide you instead of your ego.

_____

_____

_____

_____

_____

_____

_____

_____

_____

_____

_____

• • •

Playing with Life's Passion To discover things you're passionate about, try embracing your inner child. Be adventuresome and try new things. Happiness research shows that trying new things increases dopamine levels in the brain, which contributes to sustained levels of contentment.

Today Give yourself permission to be a kid. Think of something frivolous you would enjoy doing but that is not important. Write about this. How long have you thought this would be interesting?

_____

_____

_____

_____

_____

_____

_____

_____

_____

_____

• • •

Based on a True Story Here's a fun way to help you stop focusing on difficulties in your past. Slightly rewrite your life story by emphasizing the positive things and skimming over the negatives.

Today Write the highlights of your new life story. Pretend you're pitching it to a Hollywood producer.

_____

_____

_____

_____

_____

_____

_____

_____

_____

_____

_____

_____

● ● ●

To Support a Change Is there a part of your life you'd like
to improve? Look around for groups that meet to talk about
this topic. Plan on making a good first impression: smile and
introduce yourself, use open body language, and ask people's
names.

Today What type of meet-up group would interest you?

_____

_____

_____

_____

_____

_____

_____

_____

_____

_____

_____

• • •

Subtraction Is Good Math Professor of psychology Robert Emmons at the University of California, Davis, suggests imagining your life without certain blessings.

Gratitude Day Today, think about what your life would be like without one particular blessing. But to stay positive, write about how grateful you are to have this blessing in your life.

_____

_____

_____

_____

_____

_____

_____

_____

_____

_____

_____

• • •

Say Thank You Research shows that when we say "thank you" out loud, it helps us to declare our positive feelings, which in turn makes us happy.

(Reminder: tomorrow is Kindness Day.)

Today Write about how you plan to say "thank you" to a loved one and express how you're so glad to have them in your life.

_____

_____

_____

_____

_____

_____

_____

_____

_____

_____

_____

● ● ●

Altruism and Kindness Scientists have shown that altruistic behavior releases endorphins in the brain, producing the positive feeling known as the "helper's high."

Today Write about one kind act you did recently and how it made you feel.

_____

_____

_____

_____

_____

_____

_____

_____

_____

_____

❑ Kindness Day Did you do three acts of kindness in the last 24 hours?

● ● ●

Something to Increase Professor Lyubomirsky, author of
The How of Happiness, talks about what the happiest people
do. The happiest people spend a lot of time with family and
friends and know it's important to work on these relationships.

Today Write about the relationship you would like to improve
in the next 24 hours.

_____

_____

_____

_____

_____

_____

_____

_____

_____

_____

• • •

Open Up to Optimism The happiest people have an optimistic perspective when they think about the future.

Today Pick one area of your life, ignore any pessimistic feelings, and write about the brightest, most optimistic future you can think of for yourself in this area.

_____

_____

_____

_____

_____

_____

_____

_____

_____

_____

_____

_____

● ● ●

Here and Now The happiest people pay attention to the present moment. Focus your attention on right now. Don't think about anything in the past or in the future.

Today Write about what's happening right now. How do you feel?

_____

_____

_____

_____

_____

_____

_____

_____

_____

_____

_____

_____

• • •

Savor Five Ways The happiest people savor life's pleasures.
This can involve any of your senses.

Today For each of your senses (taste, touch, smell, sight, and
hearing) write about one thing you would like to savor.

_____

_____

_____

_____

_____

_____

_____

_____

_____

_____

_____

_____

_____

● ● ●

More Than Thank You The happiest people don't hesitate to be thankful for all they have in their life. They count their blessings and readily express their gratitude.

Gratitude Day Write about three things you saw or experienced that you are especially grateful for this week.

_____

_____

_____

_____

_____

_____

_____

_____

_____

_____

_____

_____

• ● •

Always Aspiring Professor Lyubomirsky says the happiest people aspire to goals that are consistent with their personal values. They enjoy mastering the steps along the way.

(Reminder: tomorrow is Kindness Day.)

Today Write about one thing you aspire to do. What are the steps you envision?

_____

_____

_____

_____

_____

_____

_____

_____

_____

_____

_____

• • •

Something to Give Away The happiest people practice kindness by offering help to neighbors, coworkers, and even strangers.

Today Write about a time when you helped a neighbor.

_____

_____

_____

_____

_____

_____

_____

_____

_____

_____

_____

❑ Kindness Day Did you do three acts of kindness in the last 24 hours?

● ● ●

Video to Real Life Jane McGonigal, game designer and author of *SuperBetter*, says using a power-up in your life, like in a video game, can be considered doing something that gives you strength, happiness, or pleasure.

Today Pretend you have acquired a power-up to get you through a difficult task. Name your power-up and write about what task you will use it with. Keep it in your back pocket to fortify your confidence.

_____

_____

_____

_____

_____

_____

_____

_____

_____

_____

● ● ●

Hearing Power-Up You can use a real world power-up to help you with a difficult task or through challenging times.

Today A power-up can sing to you. What three songs make you feel powerful?

_____

_____

_____

_____

_____

_____

_____

_____

_____

_____

_____

_____

_____

• • •

Body Power-Up When you're going through a difficult time, it often helps to quickly drop everything and do a power-up exercise.

Today What exercise would be a power-up for you that takes less than 20 minutes?

_____

_____

_____

_____

_____

_____

_____

_____

_____

_____

_____

_____

• ○ •

Reading Power-Up Reading a book or magazine that inspires you can be a great power-up activity.

Today What book or magazine can you keep near your bedside to reach for when you want a power-up? Come to think of it, you can use this journal as a reading power-up, too.

_____

_____

_____

_____

_____

_____

_____

_____

_____

_____

_____

_____

● ● ●

Recall Power-Up Studies have shown positive results if you recall a memory that makes you feel happy and satisfied and then savor it for 30 seconds. This would be considered a super power-up activity.

Gratitude Day What's the first power-up memory that comes to mind? Does this make you feel grateful?

_____

_____

_____

_____

_____

_____

_____

_____

_____

_____

_____

_____

● ○ ●

Picture Power-Up A photo or video can often create a quick moment of connection or pleasure for you.

(Reminder: tomorrow is Kindness Day.)

Today Write about a photo or video that always makes you smile.

_____

_____

_____

_____

_____

_____

_____

_____

_____

_____

_____

_____

_____

● ● ●

Kindness Power-Up Jane McGonigal says doing a small thing for others is considered to be a power-up activity that benefits you as well as them.

Today Write about a small thing you can do for someone this week.

_____

_____

_____

_____

_____

_____

_____

_____

_____

_____

❏ Kindness Day Did you do three acts of kindness in the last 24 hours?

• • •

Habit Power-Up Sometimes there's a daily habit that just makes you feel great when you remember to do it. This positive emotion will add to your power-up feeling of control.

Today What daily habit is this for you? No, you can't say brushing your teeth! Make it something more significant than that.

_____

_____

_____

_____

_____

_____

_____

_____

_____

_____

_____

_____

● ● ●

Space Power-Up Do you have a place you go to that gives you comfort or joy? Going there will give you that power-up feeling of control.

Today What power-up place gives you a feeling of comfort and joy?

_____

_____

_____

_____

_____

_____

_____

_____

_____

_____

_____

● ● ●

Lovely weather so far;
I don't know how long it
will last, but I'm not afraid
of storms, for I'm learning
how to sail my ship.

LOUISA MAY ALCOTT,
Little Women (1868–69)

Person Power-Up In order to get a power-up feeling of control, Jane McGonigal suggests thinking of someone who would be the best person to call, text, write, or visit to get a quick pick-me-up.

Today Who's the best person to call or text today who would give you that power-up feeling of pleasure? Don't delay.

_____

_____

_____

_____

_____

_____

_____

_____

_____

_____

_____

• • •

Gaming Challenge Jane McGonigal says that, to become happier and to achieve our goals, we need to do things that are difficult for us to face. But in order to do so, we need to be open to failing and trying again.

Today If your life were a game, what would be one of the bad guys you would have to face? Perhaps it's television, sweets, or maybe an actual video game?

_____

_____

_____

_____

_____

_____

_____

_____

_____

_____

• • •

Small Challenges Get into a positive mindset and say, "Yes, I'm up for a challenge!" Think of three habits you would like to break.

Gratitude Day What is one habit you've broken and are grateful for doing so?

_____

_____

_____

_____

_____

_____

_____

_____

_____

_____

_____

_____

● ● ●

Challenging a Habit Think about the number-one habit you want to break; if it's a biggie, do you need to call in reinforcements?

(Reminder: tomorrow is Kindness Day.)

Today Do you need to call in a friend or a mentor to help you with this habit? What's the first step you can take?

_____

_____

_____

_____

_____

_____

_____

_____

_____

_____

_____

● ● ●

Buy Some Happiness Yes, you *can* buy happiness when it's for other people. You could buy a trip, tickets to a concert, or a special dinner out for people close to you. This provides happiness for them and for you as well.

Today What would you like to buy for someone?

_____

_____

_____

_____

_____

_____

_____

_____

_____

_____

_____

❏ **Kindness Day** Did you do three acts of kindness in the last 24 hours?

● ● ●

Don't Sabotage Success By managing your body language, you can change others' perception of you. If you don't manage it, you might be sabotaging your own success. When you stand straight, with your shoulders back and head held high, you look self-assured and confident.

Today Write about how you're going to manage your body language the next time you want to look especially self-assured.

_____

_____

_____

_____

_____

_____

_____

_____

_____

_____

_____

• • •

Less Stress By managing your body language, you're sending a message to your brain to strengthen positive and confident feelings. Confident body language not only makes you *look* self-assured; it actually makes you *feel* more self-assured as well.

Today Recall a time when you walked into a room where people looked at you and you felt confident.

_____

_____

_____

_____

_____

_____

_____

_____

_____

_____

_____

_____

● ● ●

We're Looking! Note how you're sitting right now. Are you slumped in a chair with your head forward and your back bent? Try sitting with your rear all the way back against the chair, with you knees bent and your feet flat on the floor. This puts the least amount of stress on your muscles and your ligaments. Try to check yourself during the day when you're busy and stressed.

Today Do the above positive suggestion and write down whether or not it made you feel better.

_____

_____

_____

_____

_____

_____

_____

_____

_____

_____

● ● ●

Time to Smile When you want to reduce stress, here's what to do: smile. Even if you're working at your desk or driving your car—smile. Smiling releases endorphins, which combat stress hormones. You should practice smiling right now even if you feel foolish. When's the next time you should remember to smile? How about when you're driving your car in heavy traffic?

Today How's this smile making you feel right now?

_____

_____

_____

_____

_____

_____

_____

_____

_____

• • •

For Your Body Gratitude can improve your physical health as well as your mental health and happiness. Do your body a favor by practicing gratitude. It can involve a big thing, such as appreciating your family, or something little, such as being grateful for a compliment.

Gratitude Day Write about one big thing and two little things that make you grateful.

_____

_____

_____

_____

_____

_____

_____

_____

_____

_____

_____

● ● ●

Buying Happiness Elizabeth Dunn, coauthor of *Happy Money*, says money *can* buy happiness. It's not how much money you have, but rather what you spend it on, that matters. The human brain loves surprises, so buying someone a surprise gift is buying them happiness. Elizabeth also says that spending money on others is buying you happiness. By combining the two, your brain will become even happier.

(Reminder: tomorrow is Kindness Day.)

Today Think about surprising a friend with tickets to a special event or even with a gift. What will you get?

_____

_____

_____

_____

_____

_____

_____

_____

• • •

Light Up Your Brain A study at the University of Oregon shows that four areas of the brain light up when people perform charity work. To keep it simple, let's say these are the feel-good parts of the brain. It's especially strong if the charity work is voluntary.

Today Write about a time when you donated time or money. How did it make you feel?

_____

_____

_____

_____

_____

_____

_____

_____

_____

❑ Kindness Day Did you do three acts of kindness in the last 24 hours?

● ● ●

Is That Wonder Woman? Harvard body-language research demonstrates that if you take the Wonder Woman or Batman pose for two minutes before a stressful situation, it reduces the amount of cortisol, a stress hormone, in your system. This is the pose with your hands on your hips, feet wide apart, and shoulders back, looking straight ahead.

Today Try the pose. How do you feel? When's the next time you can use it to your advantage?

_____

_____

_____

_____

_____

_____

_____

_____

_____

_____

● ● ●

Wonder Woman Persuades Now that you have the strong Wonder Woman or Batman pose in mind, you may want to use it to persuade someone. Take the communication advice of Dianna Booher, communications expert and author of *What More Can I Say?* She says saying "Yes, but" in a conversation immediately puts the other person on the defensive. Saying "Yes, and" moves the conversation in a more positive direction.

Today Write about a situation you'd like to improve by using this positive approach.

_____

_____

_____

_____

_____

_____

_____

_____

_____

_____

● ● ●

Aligned Willpower It's easy to pick a goal you believe others think you should want. It's more important to look deeply within and pick something truly important to you.

Today Write about one such goal and why it's so important to you.

_____

_____

_____

_____

_____

_____

_____

_____

_____

_____

_____

_____

• • •

Weightlifting Willpower The good news is that you can increase your willpower by lifting weights. Well, not real weights, but you can increase your willpower by taking small steps toward your goal.

Today What's the first small step you can take toward your aligned willpower goal? This is a goal that's very important to your life.

_____

_____

_____

_____

_____

_____

_____

_____

_____

_____

_____

● ● ●

Get a Higher Return By practicing gratitude, you can expect higher levels of positive emotions. Studies by Professor Robert Emmons show that you can increase your positivity by 25 percent by practicing gratitude. Now that's a big plus, isn't it?

Gratitude Day Today you can benefit from gratitude. List three things from the last 24 hours that you're grateful for.

_____

_____

_____

_____

_____

_____

_____

_____

_____

_____

• ○ •

Mindless Diversification Scott Barry Kaufman, coauthor of *Wired to Create*, advises you to take a break while working on a task with a pause for mindless activity. When you take a break for mindlessness or daydreaming, your attention has been expanded and your mind is able to make more creative connections between ideas.

(Reminder: tomorrow is Kindness Day.)

Today Write about a mindless activity that works for you. Yes, taking a bath and paying attention to the creative ideas that "bubble up" counts.

_____

_____

_____

_____

_____

_____

_____

_____

_____

_____

• • •

Be Generous Giving without expecting anything in return gives you something—a dose of feel-good hormones. Plus, when you give, you often start a pay-it-forward wave of generosity, making the world a little better.

Today Write about new thoughtful things you can do for others. Your brain loves novelty; it wakes up and pays more attention.

_____

_____

_____

_____

_____

_____

_____

_____

_____

❑ **Kindness Day** Did you do three acts of kindness in the last 24 hours? If you're especially proud of one, add it to your Kindness Treasures page at the end of this journal.

● ● ●

Charisma Olivia Fox Cabane, author of *The Charisma Myth*, says you can increase your charisma when meeting someone new by giving them your complete attention. Be truly present and listen. Then make your exit memorable. You can do this by mentioning a book, a website, or even a person you can introduce to them.

Today Write about a time when you met someone, and really connected and made a memorable exit by recommending something they would like.

_____

_____

_____

_____

_____

_____

_____

_____

_____

_____

● ● ●

Charisma Crumbler Cabane says the biggest inhibitor to charisma is self-doubt, which shows up as imposter syndrome. If
you've had this feeling, you're not alone. Each year, the incom-
ing class of the Stanford Business School is asked, "Please raise
your hand if you feel like you're the one mistake the admis-
sions committee made." Each year, two thirds of the class raise
their hands.

Today Write about what you'd say to one of those students.
Now use this advice the next time you feel like an imposter.

_____

_____

_____

_____

_____

_____

_____

_____

_____

_____

● ● ●

Quick Charisma Expansion Follow the advice of Cabane, who says to "stare like a lover, stand like a gorilla, and speak like a preacher." You want deep but warm eye contact, a stance that broadcasts power and confidence, and to speak in a slow, confident, resonant, and warm voice.

Today Which charismatic person comes to mind who uses these techniques?

_____

_____

_____

_____

_____

_____

_____

_____

_____

_____

● ● ●

Norma Jean or Marilyn Monroe In *The Charisma Myth*, Cabane relates a story about Marilyn Monroe in 1955. As an experiment, Marilyn took a photographer with her to Grand Central Station in New York. She walked through the busy crowd in a quiet manner, and no one seemed to notice her. Then she fluffed her hair, changed her stance, and took on a new persona as she walked through the crowd again. She became magnetic, and everyone suddenly seemed to notice her.

Today Conduct your own experiment in the next 24 hours and assume a magnified persona. Be creative and give this alter ego a name. You'll be surprised at the results!

_____

_____

_____

_____

_____

_____

_____

_____

_____

• • •

Write About It Gratitude journaling about people benefits you greatly. It affects your health and happiness in positive ways.

Gratitude Day Write about three people who had a positive impact on your childhood.

_____

_____

_____

_____

_____

_____

_____

_____

_____

_____

_____

_____

_____

● ● ●

Learned Charisma As you're experimenting with increasing your charisma, go easy on yourself. Don't expect a big change immediately, but rather look at each little change to see what's working. Remember, it doesn't change who you are as a person; it changes how other people perceive you.

(Reminder: tomorrow is Kindness Day.)

Today Write about how you want to be perceived by others.

_____

_____

_____

_____

_____

_____

_____

_____

_____

_____

_____

• • •

Helping Your Health Research shows that your immune system can be improved by doing acts of kindness. During periods of stress, our brain's fight-or-flight response goes into overdrive, which can be counterbalanced by neurochemical processes associated with acts of kindness. This is very important to your health and well-being, and we'll be going into this further in future weeks.

Today Write about how important doing acts of kindness are to your well-being.

_____

_____

_____

_____

_____

_____

_____

_____

❏ **Kindness Day** Did you do three acts of kindness in the last 24 hours?

● ● ●

Watching a Movie Picture yourself in a theater, watching a movie of your best possible future five years from now. See yourself happy with all of your goals realized. Imagine it in fine detail and feel all of the emotions. We will revisit this scenario in various ways.

Today Write about what you saw and how you felt.

_____

_____

_____

_____

_____

_____

_____

_____

_____

_____

● ● ●

Listen to It Yesterday you were watching a movie of your best possible future five years from now. You should thank someone who helped you: your inner cheerleader. This voice is so important. It builds your confidence and guides you around obstacles. Listen to it and turn up the volume.

Today Write about what your inner cheerleader says to you when the negative voice is undermining your confidence.

_____

_____

_____

_____

_____

_____

_____

_____

_____

_____

_____

● ● ●

Decision Time Life coach Jaime Kulaga says that when you feel challenged, reflect on your overall successes in life and then look at positive choices you've made recently. You should feel confident that you are capable of succeeding with new feats in the present.

Today Write about three positive choices or decisions you've made in the past week.

_____

_____

_____

_____

_____

_____

_____

_____

_____

_____

_____

● ● ●

Happiness Guide Shawn Achor, who Oprah acknowledges as her happiness guru, says he subscribes to the ancient Greeks' definition of happiness: "the joy you feel when striving toward your potential." In the science of happiness, we're not studying fleeting pleasure but a greater, more important sense of joy and fulfillment.

Today What one specific thing does "striving toward your potential" bring to mind for you?

_____

_____

_____

_____

_____

_____

_____

_____

_____

_____

• • •

Focus on People Journaling about people for whom you're grateful has more of an impact than focusing on the things that make you grateful.

Gratitude Day Make today's gratitude journaling about a particular person.

_____

_____

_____

_____

_____

_____

_____

_____

_____

_____

_____

_____

● ● ●

Quick Guide to Happiness Follow Achor's quick guide to happiness right now:

- *Spend two minutes meditating, even if it's merely feeling your breath going in and out.*
- *Write a list of three unique things that make you grateful.*
- *Spend two minutes journaling about a positive experience.*
- *Spend two minutes writing a positive e-mail to send to someone.*

(Reminder: tomorrow is Kindness Day.)

Today Since this is a five-minute journal, you may want to pick three of the four above.

_____

_____

_____

_____

_____

_____

_____

_____

_____

_____

● ● ●

Kindness by Sonja Professor Lyubomirsky found that people were much happier when she asked them to perform acts of kindness one day each week instead of daily. Most people become bored with the same focus every day. Of course they'll be kind, but the focus loses its glitter and their brains habituate.

Today Write about if you're the type of person who does better with a once-a-week focus.

_____

_____

_____

_____

_____

_____

_____

_____

_____

❏ **Kindness Day** Did you do three acts of kindness in the last 24 hours?

• • •

Four Happy Chemicals Dr. Loretta Breuning, author of *Habits of a Happy Brain,* talks about our four "happy-brain chemicals," each of which motivates a different type of survival behavior. The chemicals are: dopamine, the joy of finding what you seek; endorphin, the oblivion that masks pain; oxytocin, the comfort of social alliances; and serotonin, the security of social importance. Let's talk today about forming new dopamine habits. Start celebrating your daily small successes to trigger the dopamine chemical.

Today Write about one small success that happened recently.

_____

_____

_____

_____

_____

_____

_____

_____

_____

• • •

Chemistry of Laughter A true fit of laughter triggers endorphins in your body. Dr. Breuning says that laughter releases fear. Imagine laughing with relief after a close call with a snake. Make it a point to find a type of comedy that gives you a true endorphin laugh.

Today What comedian or type of comedy always makes you laugh? Try laughing at this once a day when you're stressed.

_____

_____

_____

_____

_____

_____

_____

_____

_____

_____

_____

● ● ●

Trusting Oxytocin When you trust a friend and a friend trusts you, the chemical oxytocin is triggered. You can enjoy more oxytocin by creating opportunities for people to trust you.

Today Write about a trusting relationship that you've enjoyed.

_____

_____

_____

_____

_____

_____

_____

_____

_____

_____

_____

_____

_____

_____

• • •

Serotonin Pride Dr. Breuning says that serotonin is the chemical of social importance. She advises you to simply enjoy when others have followed your lead and appreciate your good effect on others.

Today Write about your subtle influence on someone so you can feel a slight surge of serotonin.

_____

_____

_____

_____

_____

_____

_____

_____

_____

_____

_____

_____

● ● ●

Write or Think? Research shows that writing about things you're grateful for has a much stronger emotional impact than merely speaking or thinking them.

Gratitude Day Today, grab a pen and write in depth about one thing that makes you grateful.

_____

_____

_____

_____

_____

_____

_____

_____

_____

_____

_____

_____

● ● ●

Behavior and Biochemistry Create micromoments of mutual caring, whether it's with a friend, a neighbor, or even a stranger; send the positive chemical oxytocin through your system by looking into their eyes.

(Reminder: tomorrow is Kindness Day.)

Today Decide to have a micromoment with someone in the next 24 hours. Who's it going to be? Remember to look into their eyes.

_____

_____

_____

_____

_____

_____

_____

_____

_____

_____

• • •

Volunteer for Kindness A study led by Doug Oman of University of California, Berkeley found that when elderly people volunteered with more than one organization, they were 44 percent less likely to die over a five-year period than those who did not volunteer. Even if you're not elderly, it can still help you.

Today Write about a time when you volunteered.

_____

_____

_____

_____

_____

_____

_____

_____

_____

_____

❏ Kindness Day Did you do three acts of kindness in the last 24 hours?

● ● ●

Move Quickly from One To-Do to the Next? When your mind is focused on the future, you're less happy and less productive. Instead, keep your mind on the task or conversation at hand. You'll be happier and more charismatic.

Today Write about how you'll remind yourself to stay in the present. It can be a word or phrase.

_____

_____

_____

_____

_____

_____

_____

_____

_____

_____

_____

_____

• • •

Belly Breathing for Less Stress? More than 80 percent of doctor visits occur because we often operate in a high-stress state. A deep abdominal breathing exercise can help reduce stress. Sit up straight and put both hands on your stomach. Inhale deeply through your nose, filling your abdomen so that you feel your hands rise. Exhale through your mouth, pushing out all the air while contracting your stomach muscles. Reduce your stress with one or two breaths.

Today Take two relaxing breaths now and write about how it made you feel. Do you feel more relaxed? Do you think you should try this the next time you're overstressed?

_____

_____

_____

_____

_____

_____

_____

_____

_____

● ● ●

Persevere at All Costs? Instead of pushing yourself to the limit and depleting your body, realize that taking a little time for yourself is saving energy for your body.

Today Write about what you can do with this little break.

_____

_____

_____

_____

_____

_____

_____

_____

_____

_____

_____

_____

_____

● ● ●

Always Stay Focused on Your Work? Research shows that taking a little time off from focusing on your work actually makes you more creative and gives you new insights—you know, those aha moments.

Today Write about one time when you were unfocused and had an aha moment.

_____

_____

_____

_____

_____

_____

_____

_____

_____

_____

_____

_____

• • •

Do More Math When you did "Subtraction Is Good Math" in a Week 8, Day 5, you had to imagine your life without certain blessings. For this exercise, consider all the blessings in your life.

Gratitude Day Write about three wonderful blessings that you're glad you don't have to do without.

_____

_____

_____

_____

_____

_____

_____

_____

_____

_____

_____

• • •

Think Work Many people are most productive in the late mornings. Does this sound like you? Christine Carter, author of *The Sweet Spot,* advises you to pick a specific time slot, and shut down your e-mail and any distracting windows or apps. Carter also suggests aiding concentration by listening to music that's not distracting. Music helps us concentrate on the work at hand and increases our energy.

(Reminder: tomorrow is Kindness Day.)

Today What time of day will you do your hard work? What are the first five songs you want to have on your work playlist?

_____

_____

_____

_____

_____

_____

_____

_____

_____

_____

● ● ●

Snowball It When we give to others, we can spur a snowball effect with the recipient and anyone observing. Each person can impact dozens and even hundreds of people in a network. An entire community can benefit when we give.

Today Write about a snowball effect that you would love to start. It can be as easy as paying for someone's coffee.

_____

_____

_____

_____

_____

_____

_____

_____

_____

_____

❏ **Kindness Day** Did you do three acts of kindness in the last 24 hours?

● ● ●

Ten Talking Tips Journalist and talk-show host Celeste Headlee gives advice on how to have a great conversation in 10 easy steps. The first tip is *listen*. If you are speaking as the other person is speaking, you're not learning and not focusing on the conversation. The second tip is *don't multitask*. It's not only about putting your phone down. Try to focus on the conversation and be in the moment.

Today Write about a conversation you enjoyed.

_____

_____

_____

_____

_____

_____

_____

_____

_____

_____

● ● ●

To Sway or Not to Sway? The third talking tip is *don't pon-tificate*. Don't use the conversation as a chance to convert the other person to your opinion. You know how you feel when someone does this to you. Give them a chance to state their beliefs, and see if you might learn something new.

Today Write about a time when you had a conversation that went into an interesting or surprising new territory.

_____

_____

_____

_____

_____

_____

_____

_____

_____

_____

● ● ●

Be a Journalist The fourth talking tip is *use open-ended questions*. Take a lesson from journalists and start your questions with *who, what, when, where, why,* or *how*. It minimizes the chance of getting a boring *yes* or *no* response.

Today Write about someone you could ask, "What's the most surprising thing you've come across in your field, job, or neighborhood?"

_____

_____

_____

_____

_____

_____

_____

_____

_____

_____

● ● ●

Go with the Flow and Admit It The fifth talking tip is *go with the flow*, which means that even though a random thought just popped into your head that has nothing to do with the topic at hand, don't let it occupy your mind.

The sixth talking tip is *admit that you don't know*. Don't tell a lie when you don't know something. Be honest and say, "I don't know."

Today Write about someone you'll be talking with soon. What would you like to ask them?

_____

_____

_____

_____

_____

_____

_____

_____

_____

_____

● ● ●

Me, Too The seventh talking tip is a tough one. When someone talks about a problem with a family member or a difficult situation at work, *don't say*, "I've had the same thing happen to me." This is not about you, and no two people's experiences are the same. Let's get on to a positive note here—what can you say to keep the conversation going? How about "How did you feel?" Think like a therapist and write about what else you can say.

Gratitude Day Improve your health and happiness by writing about three things you noticed in the last 24 hours for which you're grateful.

_____

_____

_____

_____

_____

_____

_____

_____

_____

● ● ●

Once Is Enough and Avoid Weeds The eighth talking tip is
don't repeat yourself. Sometimes we repeat ourselves to make a
point, but it isn't necessary. The ninth step is to *stay out of the
weeds*. People do not generally care about small details like the
names of places or people. They care more about who you are
as a person and what you both might have in common. So stay
away from minor details.

(Reminder: tomorrow is Kindness Day.)

Today What are a few comments you can use when you need
to stop struggling with details? How about including a humorous one?

_____

_____

_____

_____

_____

_____

_____

_____

_____

● ● ●

Like a Miniskirt The tenth talking tip is *be brief*. As Franklin D. Roosevelt once advised his son, who was preparing to speak publicly, "Be sincere, be brief, be seated."

Today Write about a quick conversation you've had that was interesting. Where were you?

_____

_____

_____

_____

_____

_____

_____

_____

_____

_____

❏ **Kindness Day** Did you do three acts of kindness in the last 24 hours?

● ● ●

Open Mind Benefit #1 Dani DiPirro, author of *The Positively Present Guide to Life*, has excellent advice about having an open mind. Even though you may think the beliefs and values you learned as you were growing up are the best, having this belief limits you. Dani says opening your mind to new ideas allows you the opportunity to change what you think and how you view the world. Now, this doesn't mean you necessarily will change your beliefs, but you have the option to when you think with an open mind. Today, choose to have an open mind, release control, and experience the world without limits.

Today Write about a time when you met someone who had different beliefs and allowed yourself to think with an open mind during the conversation. Did you think there was something more you should explore?

_____

_____

_____

_____

_____

_____

_____

• • •

Open Mind Benefit #2 Have you ever experienced something new because of another person? Hopefully this was a positive experience.

Today Write about what you experienced. Are you glad you allowed yourself to have an open mind?

_____

_____

_____

_____

_____

_____

_____

_____

_____

_____

_____

● ● ●

Open Mind Benefit #3 Have you ever had an open mind and allowed yourself to be with someone who had negative values? Perhaps they were rude or unethical.

Today Write about how great this made you feel about your positive values. Surprise! You can benefit from the negative.

_____

_____

_____

_____

_____

_____

_____

_____

_____

_____

_____

• • •

Open Mind Benefit #4 Most of us don't like to show when we aren't familiar with something. It makes us feel weak and vulnerable. Be open to learning new things.

Today Write about a time when you said, "I don't know anything about that. Tell me about it," and learned something new.

_____

_____

_____

_____

_____

_____

_____

_____

_____

_____

_____

_____

● ● ●

Open Mind Benefit #5 If you don't experience new things, you can't strengthen who you are. Having new experiences either validates your current beliefs, or allows you to change them for the better.

Gratitude Day List three small things you're grateful for this week.

_____

_____

_____

_____

_____

_____

_____

_____

_____

_____

_____

_____

• • •

Open Mind Benefit #6 When you're open-minded and learn something new, you can often see the mistakes you made in the past. Accept that mistakes are part of living and that you can't grow without them. Pat yourself on the back for having made a mistake and now realizing how you can do things differently.

(Reminder: tomorrow is Kindness Day.)

Today Write about one area of your life where you plan to be more open-minded.

_____

_____

_____

_____

_____

_____

_____

_____

_____

_____

● ● ●

Open Mind Benefit #7 Being open-minded allows you to be a more confident person. It strengthens your own values and allows you to recognize others as well.

Today Write about what topic you could begin trying to be more open-minded about. I know it's tough to admit!

_____

_____

_____

_____

_____

_____

_____

_____

_____

_____

❑ **Kindness Day** Did you do three acts of kindness in the last 24 hours?

● ● ●

Willpower "I Will" Challenge Kelly McGonigal, Stanford
health psychologist and author of *The Willpower Instinct*, says
you can definitely increase your willpower. You can use her
"I will, I won't, I want" challenge. One of the first steps is to
decide what's the one thing you want to do more of that will
improve your life.

Today What is the "I will" you need to do to improve your life?

_____

_____

_____

_____

_____

_____

_____

_____

_____

_____

_____

● ● ●

Willpower "I Won't" Challenge McGonigal says you need to pinpoint one of your difficult habits that is hard to break. Is it harming your health, happiness, or success?

Today What's the "I won't" you need to stop to improve your life?

_____

_____

_____

_____

_____

_____

_____

_____

_____

_____

_____

_____

● ● ●

Willpower "I Want" Challenge Finishing up with McGonigal's willpower challenge, what long-term goal would you like to give all of your focus to?

Today Describe your "I want" in strong visual terms. Think of it as a big positive magnet pulling you in the correct direction for your life.

_____

_____

_____

_____

_____

_____

_____

_____

_____

_____

_____

_____

● ● ●

Willpower Role Model A great head start is to find someone who has already accomplished what you want to do.

Today Is there someone you know who has done what you want to do? If not, is there someone you can read about who has accomplished this goal?

_____

_____

_____

_____

_____

_____

_____

_____

_____

_____

_____

_____

● ● ●

Willpower Support It's a big help if you have family or friends who can support you in your goal. Change is easier with others.

Gratitude Day Write about who can give you positive support.

_____

_____

_____

_____

_____

_____

_____

_____

_____

_____

_____

Bonus Gratitude List three small things you're grateful for this week.

● ● ●

Willpower When Most people have more energy for their goals in the morning. In the afternoon, fatigue usually starts to build. Work toward your goal when the time is best for you.

(Reminder: tomorrow is Kindness Day.)

Today When's the best time for you? How will you schedule this into your day?

_____

_____

_____

_____

_____

_____

_____

_____

_____

_____

• • •

Stressing Your Willpower Stress and willpower do not work well together. When you're stressed, bad habits start jumping in and your brain is not focused on good decision-making. Think of what you can do to cut the stress. Perhaps five minutes of exercise or a quick walk outside can help you.

Today What's a quick stress reliever that you can do when you see you're not making headway with your goals?

_____

_____

_____

_____

_____

_____

_____

_____

_____

_____

❏ **Kindness Day** Did you do three acts of kindness in the last 24 hours?

● ● ●

Sleep on Willpower Try to get seven or eight hours of sleep each night. When you don't get enough sleep, your brain is not able to deploy energy to the most energy-expensive area of the brain, the part of the brain that handles self-control. Scientists say that's equivalent to feeling mildly intoxicated—if you happen to know what that's like.

Today How are you doing on your nightly sleep? Do you need to make any changes here?

_____

_____

_____

_____

_____

_____

_____

_____

_____

_____

_____

_____

• • •

Eating Willpower Having a balanced diet with plenty of fruits and vegetables and fewer processed foods helps strengthen your willpower. If you're having trouble with procrastination, take a look at your diet.

Today How are your diet and procrastination? Are there any changes you should make?

_____

_____

_____

_____

_____

_____

_____

_____

_____

_____

_____

● ● ●

Willpower Limits Know your limits and plan for them. Things that can limit your willpower are: getting yourself into tempting situations, giving up at the first obstacle, and not asking for help.

Today What are the willpower limits you should plan ahead for? Write about the positive things you'll do to stay on track.

_____

_____

_____

_____

_____

_____

_____

_____

_____

_____

• • •

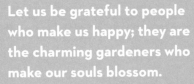

Let us be grateful to people who make us happy; they are the charming gardeners who make our souls blossom.

MARCEL PROUST,
Les Plaisirs et les Jours (1896)

Flex Your Willpower If you see that achieving a goal is not working out or you aren't creating the results you want, then you need to be open to changing the steps it takes to get there.

Today Time to give yourself a willpower boost. Write about a goal you've achieved and how great you felt while doing so.

_____

_____

_____

_____

_____

_____

_____

_____

_____

_____

_____

● ● ●

Willpower Choices Mindfulness comes into play with your willpower. According to Kelly McGonigal, one study found that the average person thinks they make 14 food choices a day but actually makes over 200. When you aren't aware that you're making a choice, you'll almost always default to habit or temptation.

Gratitude Day Write about three things you're grateful for this week.

_____

_____

_____

_____

_____

_____

_____

_____

_____

_____

_____

● ● ●

Willpower Rewards In *Habits of a Happy Brain*, Dr. Breuning says that your mammal brain constantly scans for potential rewards, and dopamine is the stimulus when you see that you're approaching a reward. In between the immediate cookies and the impossible future dream is the joy of getting a step closer. It feels good, which motivates you to keep seeking and finding. Put this information to good use and attach a healthy dopamine reward (aka: "dopamize") to things you're reluctant to do.

(Reminder: tomorrow is Kindness Day.)

Today You can be creative here. List five small rewards that would "dopaminize" your least favorite tasks.

_____

_____

_____

_____

_____

_____

_____

_____

• • •

Willpower Deserves Some Slack If you do encounter a setback, cut yourself some slack. Studies show that people who suffer from guilt or shame are more likely to give up on their goals. The next time you suffer a setback, go easy on yourself and act like a good friend.

Today Write about what you plan to do the next time you have a setback.

_____

_____

_____

_____

_____

_____

_____

_____

_____

❏ **Kindness Day** Did you do three acts of kindness in the last 24 hours? If you're especially proud of one, add it to your Kindness Treasures page at the end of this journal.

• • •

You and Future You One thing we tend to do is imagine that our future self will have more energy, will make better decisions, and will have less fear than our current self. Princeton's perception-bias expert, Emily Pronin, says this leads us to treat our future self like a stranger. Fortunately, there's a positive work-around. Let's say there's a project you're thinking of either starting now, or putting off for a month. Visualize yourself one month from now putting things together and seeing the consequences of this decision. The more vivid the future feels, the more likely you are to make a decision you'll be happy with.

Today What's a project you're thinking about starting?

_____

_____

_____

_____

_____

_____

_____

_____

• • •

Message to Future You Here's another way to avoid thinking of the future you as a stranger. Write a letter telling the
future you what you're going to do now to help reach long-
term goals. Describe how happy you think the future you will
be with the decisions you're making now.

Today Write this special letter to the future you.

_____

_____

_____

_____

_____

_____

_____

_____

_____

_____

_____

● ● ●

Imagine Positive Consequences Imagining your future self can help strengthen your current willpower. A study divided couch potatoes into two groups. The first group was asked to visualize exercising regularly and experiencing the health benefits, while the other was asked to picture not exercising and suffering the health consequences in the future. The visualizations got both groups to get up off the couch. A control group, which did not imagine a future self, did not change.

Today Let's not be negative here. Imagine your future self enjoying the results of a good new habit.

_____

_____

_____

_____

_____

_____

_____

_____

_____

● ○ ●

Date _____

Week 22 • Day 4

Have This Type of Mind Psychologist Rick Hanson says that having a "don't know mind" is the foundation of a scientist's perception of the world, or a child's, an artist's, a poet's—or even a saint's. Think about a personal interaction that's worrying you. Assume a "don't know mind" and ask yourself these questions: Am I really sure? What else could be true? What's it like for them to be on the receiving end of this? Am I getting attached to my views rather than holding them lightly?

Today What are your answers to these questions?

_____

_____

_____

_____

_____

_____

_____

_____

_____

● ● ●

The Power of Pride Social emotions probably evolved to help keep us in good standing with our tribes. You can use this human need for approval to help strengthen your will-power. Imagine how happy someone in your family—or someone in your group whose opinion matters to you—will be when you succeed.

Gratitude Day Write about one positive thing that happened in the last 24 hours.

_____

_____

_____

_____

_____

_____

_____

_____

_____

_____

● ○ ●

Avoid Hangry You know you get easily emotional and irritated when you're hungry, right? When you need to have a discussion with a friend, colleague, or family member about a touchy subject, make sure both of you are well fed before talking. Psychologist Brad Bushman explains that we have a hard time managing our anger when we're hungry. When we eat, the glucose in our meal helps the brain to balance our emotions.

(Reminder: tomorrow is Kindness Day.)

Today Write about the time of day when you're most receptive to handling an intense discussion. Specify a time range and try to direct the next conversation to then.

_____

_____

_____

_____

_____

_____

_____

_____

• • •

Light Up Research shows that charitable giving lights up parts of the brain that are stimulated when you receive money and when you think about moral issues. You're strengthening the connection between these two parts each time you make a charitable donation.

Today Write about a charitable gift that you think is important.

_____

_____

_____

_____

_____

_____

_____

_____

_____

_____

❑ **Kindness Day** Did you do three acts of kindness in the last 24 hours? They can be as simple as complimenting a stranger on their clothing or opening the door for someone.

● ● ●

Photoshop Your Self-Confidence Leo Babauta, author of *The Power of Less*, has good advice for increasing your self-confidence. First, make an effort to groom yourself and dress nicely every day. You'll look and feel successful and ready to tackle the world. In addition, he suggests you edit your mental self-image. Leo says that we have a mental picture of ourselves that determines how confident we are. But this picture isn't fixed and final. You are able to change it.

Today How would you like to edit the way you mentally see yourself? What small steps can you take to make these changes?

_____

_____

_____

_____

_____

_____

_____

_____

_____

_____

● ● ●

Add to Your Self-Confidence Try something new. Stepping out of your comfort zone expands your life and removes barriers. It lessens your fears and increases your self-confidence.

Today What is something out of your comfort zone that you can do right away? It doesn't have to be big.

_____

_____

_____

_____

_____

_____

_____

_____

_____

_____

_____

_____

• • •

Self-Confidence and Fear Do you have a fear that's limiting your life? A great remedy for this is to fake it till you make it. You'll feel more confident and the "faking" will start to become real.

Today Put on your fearless persona. What fear are you going to challenge?

_____

_____

_____

_____

_____

_____

_____

_____

_____

_____

_____

_____

• • •

Modeling Self-Confidence You can always increase your self-confidence, and here's a quick way to do that. Pick a model; someone you admire. This can be someone among your friends, family, coworkers, or even a celebrity. Watch how they move, talk, use gestures, and their posture.

Today Who's the model you picked? Describe how they project their self-confidence.

_____

_____

_____

_____

_____

_____

_____

_____

_____

_____

_____

● ● ●

Before a Stressful Situation When the thought, _Oh no, I'm dreading what's coming up_ runs through your mind, remember three of the most positive things you've accomplished in the past. Let them visually counter your fears.

Gratitude Day What are the three accomplishments you'll be thinking about?

_____

_____

_____

_____

_____

_____

_____

_____

_____

_____

_____

● ● ●

If Your Self-Confidence Takes a Hit Hold up the five-year mirror and ask yourself, "Will this even matter five years from now? Am I taking this too seriously?"

(Reminder: tomorrow is Kindness Day.)

Today Since this is your Positive Journal, write about something you've done recently that will make a difference five years from now.

_____

_____

_____

_____

_____

_____

_____

_____

_____

_____

_____

● ● ●

Watch a Movie Studies in the past focused on media as a negative influence. Recent research has shown that some movies, as well as other media, can have an uplifting and inspiring effect. Movies with positive messages can make us want to become better people and reach out to help others. Sophie Janicke, a positive-media psychologist, says that, rather than simply seeing media as a negative influence to rein in, we're beginning to understand that it has the potential to spread goodness on a wide scale.

Today Write about a movie that inspires and uplifts you.

_____

_____

_____

_____

_____

_____

_____

_____

❑ **Kindness Day** Did you do three acts of kindness in the last 24 hours?

• • •

More Than Watching a Movie Imagine you're at a theater and are one of the first people to see a movie you've been excitedly awaiting. It's a movie of your best possible future, only there's a little surprise for you; you're projected into the screen and are seeing everything through your own eyes.

Today Write about what you experienced, felt, and heard. Did you experience joy while seeing your wonderful future?

_____

_____

_____

_____

_____

_____

_____

_____

_____

_____

_____

• • •

Study Your Brain Brain scan studies show that thinking about something you're looking forward to increases your happiness.

Today Let's create an Anticipation List by listing three things you're looking forward to. You might be looking forward to a trip, a night out with friends, or even a special meal (maybe with a shared dessert—I'm thinking a cannoli).

_____

_____

_____

_____

_____

_____

_____

_____

_____

_____

_____

_____

● ● ●

Happy Anticipation Now take the first thing on your Anticipation List from yesterday's exercise and visualize it using all of your senses. Performance psychologist Michael Gervais says that the most effective imagery involves all five senses. You should be able to imagine the picture in your mind so vividly that it almost seems real.

Today Write about how you felt while mentally experiencing the first item on your Anticipation List.

_____

_____

_____

_____

_____

_____

_____

_____

_____

_____

● ● ●

Buy Some Bliss Purchasing things like televisions, clothes, and coffee machines won't make you happier overall. But Michael Norton, Harvard professor and coauthor of *Happy Money*, says that spending it on social experiences will make you happier. People are wired to become happier with social connections. Spending your money on concert tickets or on a yoga retreat with a friend makes you happier. Plus, anticipating your upcoming events adds to your happiness, so I say plan your vacations a year in advance and benefit from the anticipation.

Today What's one event you can start planning right now to enjoy with someone at a future date?

_____

_____

_____

_____

_____

_____

_____

_____

_____

_____

• • •

Stuff and More Stuff Grateful people are less materialistic because they appreciate what they have and are less fixated on acquiring more things.

Gratitude Day What are three nonmaterial things in your life that make you grateful?

_____

_____

_____

_____

_____

_____

_____

_____

_____

_____

_____

● ● ●

Time Affluence Professor Norton advises trying to shorten your work commute and to spend less time watching television. Spending more time with family and friends helps us become happier and feel more connected.

(Reminder: tomorrow is Kindness Day.)

Today Which of these appeals to you now: volunteering your time, spending less time commuting, or spending more time with family and friends?

_____

_____

_____

_____

_____

_____

_____

_____

_____

_____

• • •

Kindness and Empathy Parts of your brain that are dedicated to helping you see things from another person's perspective get strengthened when you put yourself in their shoes. So continue to exercise your empathy with kindness!

Today Write about who could be your empathy project.

_____

_____

_____

_____

_____

_____

_____

_____

_____

_____

❏ Kindness Day Did you do three acts of kindness in the last 24 hours?

● ● ●

Secret Weapon Even the happiest people have their share of
unhappy and tragic experiences. Their secret weapon is that
they learn to cope by using their strengths to build up their
resilience. One way to help you cope with a traumatic event is
to lean on others for support.

Today Write about one incident when your friends and family
helped you cope and how much you appreciated their help.

_____

_____

_____

_____

_____

_____

_____

_____

_____

_____

● ● ●

Plus and Minus Professor Lyubomirsky says the happiest people work on increasing the positivity around them while removing the negative in their lives.

Today Who is a positive person you would like to see more often? How do they make you feel?

_____

_____

_____

_____

_____

_____

_____

_____

_____

_____

_____

• • •

Negate Negative Chatter If there's a negative person you can't remove from your life, take this piece of advice that I love. Let them complain a bit and then say, "That's awful. What's the most positive thing that has happened today?" Then give them a genuine smile.

Today Who fits this description, and what will you say to them next time they start the negative chatter?

_____

_____

_____

_____

_____

_____

_____

_____

_____

_____

• • •

Envy Ads The happiest people try to avoid social comparisons.
When you see advertising that's designed to arouse a feeling of
envy or jealousy in you, observe it and think of a single word
that describes the emotion you feel. Brain scan research shows
that this makes the feeling less intense. Now visualize an exag-
gerated version of the ad to turn a negative into something
humorous.

Today What's an ad where you can see the humor in the failed
attempt to make you dwell in a negative emotion?

_____

_____

_____

_____

_____

_____

_____

_____

_____

_____

• • •

A Gift for You Learning to forgive is like giving yourself a nice big gift. Reliving bad feelings causes you to have the same type of destructive chemicals coursing through your body as when you were originally angry or resentful.

Gratitude Day Give yourself a great big gift. Decide right now to forgive someone who has caused you stress even if they don't deserve it. Forgive them because you're doing yourself a favor. Write your forgiveness message here.

_____

_____

_____

_____

_____

_____

_____

_____

_____

_____

• • •

Shine a Light You can increase your optimism by deciding to
focus on the bright side of every situation.

(Reminder: tomorrow is Kindness Day.)

Today What's a challenge you've faced recently? Is there a way
you can look on the bright side of this situation?

_____

_____

_____

_____

_____

_____

_____

_____

_____

_____

_____

_____

● ○ ●

Mirror, Mirror on the Brain Smiling is another way to spread kindness. It creates a beautiful smiling cycle in others because you're triggering brain mirror neurons.

Today Write about who you can try your smiling cycle on tomorrow. See if it works.

_____

_____

_____

_____

_____

_____

_____

_____

_____

_____

❏ **Kindness Day** Did you do three acts of kindness in the last 24 hours?

● ● ●

It's Recess Time You'll be more productive at whatever you're doing if you take a short break each hour. You could watch a funny video, eat a piece of chocolate, or drink a glass of water, and get back to work.

Today What three things would be good for you to do during this recess time?

_____

_____

_____

_____

_____

_____

_____

_____

_____

_____

● ● ●

Longer Recess Break Set aside an article you'd like to read when you need a longer break than your short recess time. When you're reading something that interests you, it energizes you and helps you be more productive afterward. Here's where I have to limit myself to only one 20-minute article!

Today Write about the article you plan to read, and when you will take the time to read it.

_____

_____

_____

_____

_____

_____

_____

_____

_____

_____

● ● ●

Lunch Recess It'll help you be more productive if you leave your work environment for lunch. Be mindful and savor the first few bites of your meal. Then let your mind wander toward positive things. This will help you become more creative.

Today Write down three positive things that you plan to think about during your next lunch break.

_____

_____

_____

_____

_____

_____

_____

_____

_____

_____

_____

_____

● ● ●

Afternoon Fatigue Most people lose energy in the afternoon. It's good to use this time for nontaxing scheduled appointments or phone calls. When your intellect is fatigued, it's hard to focus.

Today Write about an easygoing person you plan to call and what you'd like to discuss.

_____

_____

_____

_____

_____

_____

_____

_____

_____

_____

• • •

Stick Your Head Outside For your well-being, it's important to try to get outside, even briefly, in the afternoons. Author Christine Carter says that when we're stressed, going outside and looking at the natural landscape or up at the sky can calm us down. Walking outside in the daylight also slows down our melatonin production, which helps us stay focused longer.

Gratitude Day Write about two times you enjoyed yourself outside. Are you feeling more grateful now?

_____

_____

_____

_____

_____

_____

_____

_____

_____

_____

● ● ●

Game Plan Put your to-do list in game-plan order. Tell yourself
when you will complete the first task on your list. The author of
Flow, Mihaly Csikszentmihalyi, says that being aware of what
task is coming up next helps keep us focused.

(Reminder: tomorrow is Kindness Day.)

Today Write the first five things on your to-do list. Put a time
when you will finish the first item. Then write about how
you'll feel when it's completed.

_____

_____

_____

_____

_____

_____

_____

_____

_____

_____

● ● ●

Counter the Cortisol Practicing acts of kindness for others stimulates the release of the happy-brain chemical oxytocin. This chemical counteracts the stress chemical cortisol. Your mood increases and so does your desire to help.

Today Write about one kind act you did recently that gave you that happy-brain feeling.

_____

_____

_____

_____

_____

_____

_____

_____

_____

❏ **Kindness Day** Did you do three acts of kindness in the last 24 hours?

● ● ●

Doing Kevin Daum, author of *Roar!*, says that incredibly successful people understand the value of their time and possessions. They are aware of what they can accomplish with the resources they have, so they save wherever they can. For the rest of the week we'll be going through the other questions that successful people ask themselves.

Today What would you enjoy doing with the time that you've saved?

_____

_____

_____

_____

_____

_____

_____

_____

_____

_____

_____

• • •

Accomplishing Successful people ask themselves, "What's the most important thing I should accomplish today?"

Today Write about the most important thing you should accomplish in the next 24 hours and how you'll feel afterward.

_____

_____

_____

_____

_____

_____

_____

_____

_____

_____

_____

_____

● ● ●

Achieving Successful people ask themselves, "Will the steps that I'm taking now help me achieve my long-term goals?" Successful people envision their best future and set goals to achieve it.

Today What's one step you should take next week, next month, and next year to achieve your best future?

_____

_____

_____

_____

_____

_____

_____

_____

_____

_____

_____

_____

_____

• • •

Being Effective Successful people ask themselves, "What can I do to be more productive?" They want to continually become more effective in everything, from learning to communicating to leading.

Today I bet you can add to this list of things you'd like to improve. How about making new friends? Is there someone in your neighborhood or workplace you think you'd like to get to know?

_____

_____

_____

_____

_____

_____

_____

_____

_____

_____

• ● •

Having Fun Successful people ask themselves, "How can I make this enjoyable?" They know how to find the fun side to every situation or task.

Gratitude Day Write about three things that were fun for you this week.

_____

_____

_____

_____

_____

_____

_____

_____

_____

_____

_____

● ● ●

Getting Rest Successful people ask themselves, "How can I mentally give myself a break?" Kevin Daum suggests that when your brain is tired, you can take a break with some deep breathing, meditation, or even a quick walk outside.

(Reminder: tomorrow is Kindness Day.)

Today What works best for you when your brain is weary?

_____

_____

_____

_____

_____

_____

_____

_____

_____

_____

_____

● ● ●

Good for My Body? Successful people ask themselves, "Is this helpful for my physical well-being?" Physical problems can steal energy away from what you need to do to accomplish your goals. It's important to keep your body healthy so you can stay on track with your goals.

Today What do you believe is the number-one thing draining your energy?

_____

_____

_____

_____

_____

_____

_____

_____

_____

❏ Kindness Day Did you do three acts of kindness in the last 24 hours?

● ● ●

Gaming Body Challenge When we're facing challenges in a video game, we look for things to restore our energy, such as a power-up pellet or an energy boost. This concept can also be applied to your physical health. Consider a small food habit you'd like to start to improve your body.

Today For your power-up pellet, what's one food you could eat more of to improve your physical health? Now imagine that you're already stronger—what's the first step you can take?

_____

_____

_____

_____

_____

_____

_____

_____

_____

_____

• • •

Gaming Experience Challenge Jane McGonigal says to embrace negative experiences, because they will teach you a lesson and get you closer to your goal. Taking a risk here and there and being open to a failure are great steps toward being a more positive and successful person.

Today Write about if you're willing to take a risk even if it means you're open to failure. When have you done this and succeeded?

_____

_____

_____

_____

_____

_____

_____

_____

_____

_____

_____

_____

• • •

Gaming Quest Challenge Many games capture your interest by sending you on a quest, which helps structure our goals and keeps us focused. In McGonigal's *SuperBetter*, she explains that it's important to keep focused and keep moving toward our dreams. When we go on quests for our goals, we are allowing ourselves to experience our goals and desires.

Today Think about going on a quest. What's one thing you can do in the next 24 hours to give you at least one minute of living your dream?

_____

_____

_____

_____

_____

_____

_____

_____

_____

_____

• • •

Gaming Allies Challenge If you were stuck on a level in a game, a helpful thing to do would be to find at least two people who could help you with your challenges.

Today Who are two people you can talk to honestly about the challenges you face? It's great if they give you helpful advice.

_____

_____

_____

_____

_____

_____

_____

_____

_____

_____

_____

_____

● ● ●

Gaming Epic Wins Challenge Think about scoring the last-minute winning goal in soccer. When the pressure is on in a game, you envision the possibility of winning. Think about a time you came through in the final minutes on a project or challenge. How grateful did that make you feel?

Gratitude Day List three things you're grateful for this week. Remember: the more detailed you are, the better you'll feel.

_____

_____

_____

_____

_____

_____

_____

_____

_____

_____

_____

● ● ●

Gaming Heroic Identity Challenge Heroic stories inspire us
and push us forward to a better life. Adopt a secret identity.
You could be Super Mario or Beyoncé's alter ego, Sasha Fierce.

(Reminder: tomorrow is Kindness Day.)

Today Who do you choose as your heroic secret identity?

_____

_____

_____

_____

_____

_____

_____

_____

_____

_____

_____

_____

_____

• • •

Expand Your Small Talk When someone waiting on you says, "Have a good day," be ready with a reply to help brighten their day, such as "Thank you."

Today Think of a few kind things you can say to someone the next time they do something kind.

_____

_____

_____

_____

_____

_____

_____

_____

_____

_____

❑ Kindness Day Did you do three acts of kindness in the last 24 hours? Do you feel the oxytocin?

● ● ●

Video Therapy Happiness brings out the best in you in different ways. Positive emotions help you learn faster and resolve challenging situations more easily. Watching a short, funny video before handling a tough situation has been proven to help, because it puts you in a positive frame of mind.

Today What type of short, funny video can rely on the next time you're feeling stressed?

_____

_____

_____

_____

_____

_____

_____

_____

_____

_____

_____

_____

• • •

R & R Research shows that developing your positive emotions can help you recuperate from stress more quickly and become more optimistic.

Today Write about how you plan to put yourself in a positive frame of mind before you interact with a person who is usually harsh and critical.

_____

_____

_____

_____

_____

_____

_____

_____

_____

_____

● ● ●

Win-Win We used to think that, when going into any type of negotiation, you should strive to drive a tough bargain, which is a negative frame of mind. New studies show that if you have a positive frame of mind and envision a win-win solution, you will be successful much more often.

Today Write about a negotiation that worked out well for you.

_____

_____

_____

_____

_____

_____

_____

_____

_____

_____

_____

● ● ●

Step into the Upper Spiral Professor Fredrickson found that people who built up their positivity were able to cope with adversity in a more open-minded way. Her study revealed that when people have open minds, they become more positive.

Today Imagine how positivity can help you. What is the first thing that comes to mind?

_____

_____

_____

_____

_____

_____

_____

_____

_____

_____

• • •

Beyond Biases Professor Fredrickson also found that when you're experiencing positive emotions, you're more likely to look beyond racial and sexual biases. Think about a time when you were in a positive mood and were surprised by how interested you were in talking with a person who was unlike yourself.

Gratitude Day List three things that made you feel grateful this week.

_____

_____

_____

_____

_____

_____

_____

_____

_____

_____

_____

• • •

Don't Retreat Negativity causes us to retreat to protect ourselves. Having more positivity causes you to become more outgoing.

(Reminder: tomorrow is Kindness Day.)

Today Write about a time when you hesitated but then went out and socialized with others and had a great time.

_____

_____

_____

_____

_____

_____

_____

_____

_____

_____

_____

● ● ●

Say Yes Fredrickson talks about a client who had an argument
with her best friend. They had avoided each other for nine years.
One day the client received an e-mail from her friend and she
thought, "What is she contacting me for?" Rather than ignore
the situation, she decided to go ahead and say "yes" to meeting
her. When they saw each other in the parking lot. they ran to
each other and started hugging and crying.

Today Have you been involved in something like this? Or is
there someone you might want to reconcile with?

_____

_____

_____

_____

_____

_____

_____

_____

❑ **Kindness Day** Did you do three acts of kindness in the
last 24 hours? If you're especially proud of one, add it to your
Kindness Treasures page at the end of this journal.

● ● ●

Caffeine for Your Brain Researchers found that when you're
mentally exhausted, doing a task that interests you instead of
a neutral task will energize you. Even though the interesting
task is more complex and requires more effort, it motivates
you. Isn't that surprising?

Today Write about a task that recently caught your interest
and energized you. How good did it feel?

_____

_____

_____

_____

_____

_____

_____

_____

_____

_____

_____

• • •

Reduce Your Stress When your body is stressed, cortisol is released. This is your mammalian brain's way of alerting you to danger. Once you're sure there's no danger, you can begin to reduce your stress with one of the four happy-brain chemicals we talked about on Week 16, Day 1. Your plan of action should be to focus your attention elsewhere. You can do this by developing new happy habits to use when you want to reduce stress.

Today Celebrating small accomplishments triggers the happy brain chemical dopamine. Write about a series of small accomplishments you've made that can be put together like a brain movie to think about when you're on stress overload.

_____

_____

_____

_____

_____

_____

_____

_____

● ● ●

"M" for Your Mind The next time you're having trouble con-
centrating, take three minutes to meditate or "be mindful."
You can sit in a chair with your feet flat on the floor and listen
to three minutes of soft meditation music.

Today Which do you like better: meditation, or mindfulness?
Talk about a time when you've done one of these.

_____

_____

_____

_____

_____

_____

_____

_____

_____

_____

_____

_____

● ● ●

Breathe for Your Mind The next time you want to give your brain a brief nap, do a one-minute deep-breathing exercise. Breathe in for a count of two, hold for one, then breathe out for a count of four, hold for one, and repeat. The important thing to remember is to have the exhale be a longer duration than the inhale.

Today Do this for one minute and write about how great you feel!

_____

_____

_____

_____

_____

_____

_____

_____

_____

_____

● ● ●

Clear Your Mind The next time you're feeling stressed or unproductive, take four minutes to think of things that make you grateful. This will take you out of that stressed brain pattern. Think about a particular person who you feel grateful to have in your life. Make an effort to tell them how important they are to you.

Gratitude Day List three things that happened this week that you're grateful for.

_____

_____

_____

_____

_____

_____

_____

_____

_____

_____

• • •

Clear Your Mind Miracle Drug There's one "drug" you can
try where the benefits are immediate—it's called exercise.
Working out for 15 minutes on a treadmill reduces sugary crav-
ings for most people. Exercise relieves ordinary stress and is
just as powerful as an antidepressant.

(Reminder: tomorrow is Kindness Day.)

Today Write about a time exercise when made you feel great.
Can you look forward to another similar experience in the
near future?

_____

_____

_____

_____

_____

_____

_____

_____

_____

_____

● ● ●

Strengthen Your Mind Take a piece of paper and keep track of something you don't normally pay close attention to, such as what you're spending, what you're eating, how long you're exercising, or how often you're taking steps toward your goals.

Today Take a positive outlook and write about how you're proud of working on one of your goals.

_____

_____

_____

_____

_____

_____

_____

_____

_____

❏ **Kindness Day** Did you do three acts of kindness in the last 24 hours?

● ● ●

Perfect Day Imagine waking up in the morning in your perfect future. Look around the room. Take note of what you're having for breakfast. What's lined up for you that morning? Perhaps some exercise, doing your ideal type of work, talking with friends or family, or reading a book?

Today Write the details you've visualized in your perfect future day. How does this make you feel?

_____

_____

_____

_____

_____

_____

_____

_____

_____

_____

_____

• • •

Time for Bed Set up a bedtime routine that will help you relax and be ready for the next day. If you suffer from anxiety or have trouble sleeping, take a hot bath for 10 to 15 minutes. A study has shown that doing this for eight weeks is more effective and less expensive than an antidepressant for anxiety.

Today Describe your ideal bedtime routine. It may involve laying out clothes for the next day, tidying up, or perhaps reading an inspiring book.

_____

_____

_____

_____

_____

_____

_____

_____

_____

● ● ●

Smart Sleep There are a few not-so-tiny reasons you should get enough sleep. Sleep affects every part of your life, including your intelligence, relationships, moods, athletic performance, and your ability to learn and remember. Even losing 20 minutes for three days in a row can dramatically lower your IQ. Think about the amount of sleep you're currently getting and about any changes you could make to improve it.

Today What positive thing can you think about right before you go to sleep?

_____

_____

_____

_____

_____

_____

_____

_____

_____

_____

• • •

Play to Your Potential Think about what stirs your passion and what your talents are. Ask yourself if you are living up to your full potential. Should you continue on your current path? Or should you go in a new direction? This is another way to visualize your future.

Today Write about what today's prompt inspires in you.

_____

_____

_____

_____

_____

_____

_____

_____

_____

_____

_____

● ● ●

The most difficult thing is the decision to act. The rest is merely tenacity. . . . You can do anything you decide to do.

AMELIA EARHART

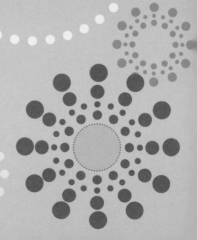

Kindness Positivity Booster Counting your blessings is a surefire way to increase your positivity.

Gratitude Day Count five little blessings in your life.

_____

_____

_____

_____

_____

_____

_____

_____

_____

_____

_____

_____

_____

● ● ●

Challenge and Flow When you find an activity that you enjoy—one that challenges you and increases your skill—you'll find yourself fully engaged in it. You'll be in a flow state.

(Reminder: tomorrow is Kindness Day.)

Today What is one activity or hobby that puts you in this flow state?

_____

_____

_____

_____

_____

_____

_____

_____

_____

_____

_____

● ● ●

Connections Whether you're socializing with old friends or getting to know new ones, just being around others and connecting increases your positivity. Dr. Fredrickson explains that even if you're not a social person but you act as if you are around others, you'll be able to garner more positivity.

Today Write about an upcoming social opportunity. Describe how you're going to handle yourself and how good you're going to feel. Will you be talkative, energetic, and have genuine concern for others? You'll begin to have more satisfying connections.

_____

_____

_____

_____

_____

_____

_____

_____

❏ Kindness Day Did you do three acts of kindness in the last 24 hours?

● ● ●

Overcoming Worry Robert Leahy, author of *The Worry Cure*, says that worriers tend to stick only with what they know and avoid new things and situations that make them uncomfortable. By not trying new things, they can avoid being uncomfortable. If worriers are able to push themselves and do things that make them uncomfortable, they will rely less on worry as a coping mechanism.

Today Write about a time when you forced yourself to do something that caused you to worry. How did you feel overcoming this?

_____

_____

_____

_____

_____

_____

_____

_____

_____

• • •

Anti-Anxious Worry Anxiety or worry is all about anticipation. The what-ifs are always much worse than what actually happens. Robert Leahy says people who worry about different scenarios think they cannot cope with those imagined situations. But on the contrary, many people are in fact able to cope with stressful and tough situations that are thrown at them.

Today Remind yourself about a time when you were really good at handling a problem.

_____

_____

_____

_____

_____

_____

_____

_____

_____

_____

• • •

Your Belly Is a Worry Buster Kathryn Tristan, author of *Why Worry?*, says a good strategy to try the next time you begin to get uneasy is to mentally tell yourself to quit worrying. She suggests belly breathing, which has been shown to calm nerves. To do this breathing exercise, put one hand on your stomach and breathe in through your nose, feeling your stomach expand. Then release the air through your mouth, keeping your tongue and jaw relaxed. As you're doing this, you'll hear a soft whooshing sound.

Today Try belly breathing now and write about how it makes you feel. Learn to value this whooshing sound as the sound of your personal relaxation.

_____

_____

_____

_____

_____

_____

_____

_____

• • •

Winning Over Worries There are two kinds of worries: productive and unproductive. For example, if you're going to take a trip, a productive worry would be, "Should I be make a reservation?" An unproductive worry would be something you have no control over, like the weather. It's counterintuitive, but writing about your worry actually lessens your stress.

Today Time to lessen your stress. Write about one worry that is unproductive and how you'll be helping yourself nip this concern in the bud next time.

_____

_____

_____

_____

_____

_____

_____

_____

_____

_____

• • •

Uncertain about Worry? Psychiatrist Bruce Levin says many worried people equate uncertainty with a bad outcome, but uncertainty is actually impartial. When you accept uncertainty, you don't have to worry anymore. Acceptance means acknowledging that uncertainty exists and letting it go, and focusing on the things that you can control, enjoy, or appreciate. For example, many people worry unnecessarily about a potential health problem in the future.

Gratitude Day Counter uncertainty about your health by writing about one positive aspect of it in a colorful way.

_____

_____

_____

_____

_____

_____

_____

_____

_____

• • •

Relieve Unhappy Chemicals Follow Dr. Breuning's advice on worrying. She says that planning is a good way to relieve unhappy chemicals. Instead of worrying all day, plan to worry only while brushing your teeth. If that's not enough, plan to worry while you floss, too.

(Reminder: tomorrow is Kindness Day.)

Today Write your worry plan now. Sometimes there's genius in simplicity.

_____

_____

_____

_____

_____

_____

_____

_____

_____

_____

• • •

Won't Need Love Repair Relationship researcher and psychologist John Gottman says those who master relationships stick to the motto: "When you're in pain, the world stops and I listen."

Today Write about a time when you stopped everything for a friend in need.

_____

_____

_____

_____

_____

_____

_____

_____

_____

_____

_____

❏ **Kindness Day** Did you do three acts of kindness in the last 24 hours?

• • •

Change What You Measure Joshua Becker, author of *The More of Less*, says that even though we know we shouldn't compare ourselves to others, we find ourselves doing it anyway. The materialistic things we find ourselves comparing, such as clothes, cars, income, beauty, or even social media followers, are not good indicators. Our self-esteem should not depend on materialistic items. Instead, he advises focusing on inner qualities, such as kindness, modesty, and love.

Today Focusing on one of these inner qualities, write about the most generous person you know.

_____

_____

_____

_____

_____

_____

_____

_____

_____

• • •

Good Competition? Author Wayne Dyer said that if you're always in a rush to get somewhere, always trying to be better than the person next to you, or motivated by another person's actions, then the person you are trying to get ahead of controls you. Instead of competing with others, how about competing with yourself?

Today What are you doing today that you couldn't have done five years ago?

_____

_____

_____

_____

_____

_____

_____

_____

_____

_____

• • •

Doggone Self-Esteem Self-esteem is under your ego's control. You know the saying by Al Franken's *Saturday Night Live* character Stuart Smalley: "I'm good enough, I'm smart enough, and doggone it, people like me." This doesn't help you deal with obstacles in life. But it does help you remember that everyone goes through hard times and can get through them.

Today Of the people you've read about who have dealt with obstacles, who do you admire most? Did they let failures stop them?

_____

_____

_____

_____

_____

_____

_____

_____

_____

• • •

Try Something New Many people won't try new things because they're afraid they could fail. I think you should give yourself a pat on the back for merely trying.

Today Write about two or three things you plan to say to yourself the next time you take a chance that doesn't work out. Please include, "At least I tried, and I'm better for it."

_____

_____

_____

_____

_____

_____

_____

_____

_____

_____

_____

• • •

Things Are Good Marianne Williamson, spiritual teacher and author of *Everyday Grace*, says that the moment we let ourselves be present and enjoy the good things around us is when we experience joy.

Gratitude Day Write about three things in your life that are really good. Get those happy chemicals moving.

_____

_____

_____

_____

_____

_____

_____

_____

_____

_____

_____

● ● ●

Power for Yourself Professor Kristin Neff, author of *Self-Compassion*, explains that great things happen when you are kind to yourself. Cutting yourself some slack doesn't mean lowering the bar or not aspiring to your goals. It's about how you think about the ups and downs of your journey. New research suggests that you're more likely to reach your goal with this process.

(Reminder: tomorrow is Kindness Day.)

Today What is something you aspire to do that may have a few setbacks along the way?

_____

_____

_____

_____

_____

_____

_____

_____

_____

_____

• • •

Friendly Talk Emma Seppälä says that many people, specifically women, are significantly kinder and more supportive to others than to themselves. We should think of how we would treat a friend who's in despair and treat ourselves the same way. We would listen to them with understanding and reassure them that mistakes are normal. We wouldn't criticize them the way we do ourselves.

Today Write about a time when you helped a friend in despair. Describe how you were able to listen and show empathy for them. Also explain how you can use the same compassion you gave your friend on yourself the next time you need it.

_____

_____

_____

_____

_____

_____

_____

❏ Kindness Day Did you do three acts of kindness in the last 24 hours?

● ● ●

Me Multitask? Author Kevin Daum says that no one is a perfect communicator. Throughout our lives, we all develop little habits and patterns. Some of these habits, such as multitasking, are not helpful. When you're talking with someone, either in person, or on the phone, they appreciate it when you give them your undivided attention.

Today Who's a person you've talked to who does the best job of giving you their undivided attention?

_____

_____

_____

_____

_____

_____

_____

_____

_____

_____

• • •

Question? Daum advises you to make it a point in every conversation to ask a couple of stimulating and related questions before the conversation is over. This will make you listen more intently to the conversation and will ensure that everyone is participating.

Today Who will you have a chance to talk to soon? What are two questions that you could ask them?

_____

_____

_____

_____

_____

_____

_____

_____

_____

_____

● ● ●

Notes Jot down notes when you're talking to someone so you can better remember the conversation. Actually writing on a piece of paper stores the information more efficiently in your brain.

Today Do you have other ideas of how you can take notes? E-mail items to yourself? Maybe taking a photo?

_____

_____

_____

_____

_____

_____

_____

_____

_____

_____

• • •

All in One Move When e-mailing someone back, make sure to respond to the entire e-mail—don't just address one thing. If you have several things to discuss, pick up the phone.

Today Instead of sending an e-mail today, how about picking up the phone? Who would be perfect to talk with?

_____

_____

_____

_____

_____

_____

_____

_____

_____

_____

_____

_____

• • •

Schedule Communications Set up a routine for replies. For example, you'll respond to a text within 20 minutes, a voice-mail within an hour, and an e-mail before you check your inbox again. Think about where you're wasting time. What would be a better schedule for you?

Gratitude Day List three things that happened this week that you're grateful for.

_____

_____

_____

_____

_____

_____

_____

_____

_____

_____

_____

• • •

Assume the Best When reading any type of communication, try to think positively. If someone seems to have a problem with you, don't assume anything—just pick up the phone. Often you may be wrong.

(Reminder: tomorrow is Kindness Day.)

Today Write about a time when you assumed something was wrong and later realized you shouldn't have relied on this assumption.

_____

_____

_____

_____

_____

_____

_____

_____

_____

_____

● ● ●

Banish Doubt When someone has sent you an e-mail and they get no reply, they may wonder if you received it or if it went to the spam folder. A good strategy is to always respond in some manner, such as "Got it" or "Thanks" or merely sending a smiley face as a quick reply. Increase your positivity right now by sending a quick e-mail to someone that will lift their spirits as well as yours.

Today Write about what quick responses you can use in the future.

_____

_____

_____

_____

_____

_____

_____

_____

❏ Kindness Day Did you do three acts of kindness in the last 24 hours?

• • •

Opposite of Self-Criticism When we compare ourselves with others, we will always find there is someone smarter, better looking, or more successful, which causes us distress. When discussing this situation, Professor Neff says to stop judging ourselves and to take the time to be nice and kind to ourselves the way we would be with others.

Today Write about how you'll talk to yourself the next time you notice you're making a comparison.

_____

_____

_____

_____

_____

_____

_____

_____

_____

_____

● ● ●

Balancing It All Life coach Jaime Kulaga says that by our very nature we are caring, nurturing, and communal. In no way should we give up these characteristics, but kindness does not equal being a doormat. Make sure to set boundaries for yourself.

Today Where do you need to set boundaries to keep people from taking advantage of your time?

_____

_____

_____

_____

_____

_____

_____

_____

_____

_____

_____

_____

• • •

Stop an Emotional Hijacking Everyone has had a time when they have gotten carried away with an emotion and said or did things they regretted. The latest research with brain scans has shown us a coping technique that works, and you'll be happy to know it's very simple. When you feel a strong emotion coming on, identify it with a simple one-word label. This lessens the fight-or-flight response and helps your brain go from an emotional state to a thinking state.

Today Name the emotions you want to reduce. Be sure to include these negative feelings: shame, envy, revenge, and jealousy. Now, let's apply a positive perspective. Write about how you feel knowing you can lessen an emotion simply by giving it a label when you feel it occurring.

_____

_____

_____

_____

_____

_____

_____

● ● ●

The Secret Key There's an unavoidable truth that everyone must face: everyone makes mistakes, including the most successful people. The key to success is learning from those mistakes and moving forward while cutting yourself some slack in the process.

Today What's something positive you learned recently after making a mistake?

_____

_____

_____

_____

_____

_____

_____

_____

_____

_____

• • •

Velcro and Teflon An easy way to raise your happiness level is to pay attention to small positives in your life and less attention to the negatives. Psychologist Rick Hanson says the brain clings to negative experiences and releases the positive ones.

Gratitude Day Write about three small positives that happened this past week.

_____

_____

_____

_____

_____

_____

_____

_____

_____

_____

● ● ●

What about My Weaknesses? Being a positive, strong, self-compassionate person does not mean ignoring your weaknesses. Everyone has them. Recognize them and know they can be changed.

(Reminder: tomorrow is Kindness Day.)

Today What is one personal weakness you're not going to ignore? What's a small change you can make in the right direction?

_____

_____

_____

_____

_____

_____

_____

_____

_____

● ● ●

Talking Game Plan We often want to keep talking, so we try to think of things to say. You might not know that the average person talks about 225 words per minute but can listen at up to 500 words per minute. So we actually have lots of time to think, and think, and get distracted.

Today Remind yourself to listen.

_____

_____

_____

_____

_____

_____

_____

_____

_____

_____

❏ **Kindness Day** Did you do three acts of kindness in the last 24 hours?

● ● ●

Savor the Future Savoring can involve thinking about the past, being mindful of the present, or considering the future, and savoring it.

Today Write about a future event you would love to have happen. Picture it—see it in your mind and savor it.

_____

_____

_____

_____

_____

_____

_____

_____

_____

_____

_____

_____

_____

• • •

Savor Meaning People who are happy and fulfilled have learned to savor the meaning of an activity.

Today What's an activity that you'll be doing in the next 24 hours that you could savor? What's does this activity mean to you?

_____

_____

_____

_____

_____

_____

_____

_____

_____

_____

_____

● ○ ●

Savor with Humor Another way to savor an activity is to incor-
porate humor into it.

Today What's an activity that you've done recently that you
can now look back on and find humor in? Doesn't this make
you feel better about mishaps?

_____

_____

_____

_____

_____

_____

_____

_____

_____

_____

_____

● ● ●

Sniffing and Savoring Your sense of smell activates one of the oldest parts of your brain. A specific scent can quickly bring out a very old memory in living color. It can be something like the scent of a campfire on your first camping trip, or the smell of a beautiful apple pie when you were a child.

Today What scent always brings a happy memory to you? Savor it now and describe your feelings.

_____

_____

_____

_____

_____

_____

_____

_____

_____

_____

_____

• • •

Savor the Touch There are so many ways that the touch of another person is beneficial. We know that touch builds trust, relationships, and can calm cardiovascular stress. A simple touch can trigger the release of oxytocin—the love hormone. Think about a touch experience that was important to you.

Gratitude Day List three beautiful things you're grateful to have in your life.

_____

_____

_____

_____

_____

_____

_____

_____

_____

_____

_____

● ● ●

Savor the Fabric Another way to savor something is to pay attention to how something feels to your touch. Have you ever watched a child with his favorite blanket? Perhaps you like the feel of a particular article of clothing.

(Reminder: tomorrow is Kindness Day.)

Today What's something you like to touch, and how does it make you feel?

_____

_____

_____

_____

_____

_____

_____

_____

_____

_____

● ● ●

Savoring the Right Thing? If you're feeling anxious, stop asking yourself questions like, "Is this the right time for this?" or "Should I be checking my e-mail now?" Take a deep breath, exhale fully, and tell yourself you're doing the perfect thing for this moment. Think about how you'll use this to curb the next stressful situation this week and how you'll pat yourself on the back when you feel your anxiety melt away.

Today Write about the perfect thing for this moment. Make sure you exhale first.

_____

_____

_____

_____

_____

_____

_____

_____

❏ **Kindness Day** Did you do three acts of kindness in the last 24 hours?

● ● ●

Anticipation and Reward Stanford neuroscientist Brian Knutson says that people report, and brain scans show, more positive arousal (or excitement) while anticipating a reward than when getting it.

Today Write about something you're anticipating, such as a future vacation or a day of relaxation.

_____

_____

_____

_____

_____

_____

_____

_____

_____

_____

_____

_____

• • •

Create Positive Pathways Since your brain created negative pathways to keep you safe, you have to add new thoughts to start building positive pathways. Surprisingly this is not as difficult as you may imagine. You merely decide you want to create a positive thought (a few times a day) when you notice a negative one. For example, traffic to work is slow today and you realize this could be a time to think a positive thought to view this in a different light: what if you didn't have a car, or didn't have public transportation, or didn't have a job? You're not ignoring the world, you're adding positive thoughts.

Today Decide you'll give this a try three times today. What three topics do you think might trigger this action? Do you think you may want to do this for more than one day?

_____

_____

_____

_____

_____

_____

_____

● ● ●

Let the Future You Thank You It's simple for people to say, "I'll do that in the future." So easy, right? A better way to handle this is to say to yourself, "What will I be missing out on in the future if I slack off now?"

Today What will the your future self appreciate you doing in the next 24 hours? Here's an advance thank-you.

_____

_____

_____

_____

_____

_____

_____

_____

_____

_____

_____

• • •

Diet Day Off A study showed that dieters who take a scheduled cheat day lost about the same amount of weight as those who stayed on their diet every single day. They also reported feeling more positive, motivated, and in control. Your diet doesn't have to be about food. It's about creating new and healthy habits. On a cheat day, you could look forward to having a couple bites of food that you avoid having most of the week, giving you the fun feeling of anticipating something triggering the dopamine in your brain.

Today Would this be a positive for you? What are three things you are looking forward to?

_____

_____

_____

_____

_____

_____

_____

_____

_____

● ● ●

Saying Thank You When someone gives you a compliment (for instance they may say, "I like your outfit"), simply say "Thank you." It may feel uncomfortable at first, but you don't need to add, "And I like your outfit, too." A simple thank-you is perfect, because it's gratifying to the person who gave you the compliment.

Gratitude Day Write about a nice compliment you've received.

_____

_____

_____

_____

_____

_____

_____

_____

_____

_____

• • •

Talk Shop If you have a particular interest you would like to pursue at work or as a hobby, choose friends you can talk shop with.

(Reminder: tomorrow is Kindness Day.)

Today Where would you like to meet with these people? A coffee shop or a restaurant?

_____

_____

_____

_____

_____

_____

_____

_____

_____

_____

_____

● ● ●

Make Me Smarter One study showed that when people spent at least 20 minutes outside, they were more open-minded and their memory spans were greater. So simply going outside can make you smarter!

Today Write about a recent time when you enjoyed being out-side and letting your mind wander.

_____

_____

_____

_____

_____

_____

_____

_____

_____

❏ **Kindness Day** Did you do three acts of kindness in the last 24 hours?

● ● ●

Your Past Doesn't Limit You Is your self-confidence being held back because of your past? It's never too late to make a change. Think of all the famous people who said they didn't start something new until they were in their forties, fifties, or sixties.

Today Picture one of your favorite late starters and write about how that inspires you to make changes for the better.

_____

_____

_____

_____

_____

_____

_____

_____

_____

_____

_____

_____

• • •

Who's Your Crowd? Surround yourself with positive people as much as possible. Being around negative people easily erodes your self-confidence.

Today Write about the three most positive people in your crowd. How do you feel when you're around them?

_____

_____

_____

_____

_____

_____

_____

_____

_____

_____

_____

_____

• • •

Not Failure When something doesn't go the way you'd planned, don't be hard on yourself. Instead, redefine it. Think of the misstep as part of a learning process. Think of it as your opportunity to improve.

Today What feedback did you recently receive about something that didn't go quite the way you expected? Has this been a positive step in your learning process?

_____

_____

_____

_____

_____

_____

_____

_____

_____

_____

_____

• • •

Your Secret Agent Training LaRae Quy, author of *Mental Toughness for Women Leaders*, is an ex-FBI agent. She talks about how important it is to be likable when you first meet someone. She says to smile immediately, ask their name, and repeat it once or twice during the conversation. She also mentions to pay attention to their facial features when they speak. As topics change, notice how their voice, animation, and body language change. Then she says to share with them the most positive things you noticed about them.

Today Now that you've begun your FBI training, what have you just learned that you want to use more often?

_____

_____

_____

_____

_____

_____

_____

_____

● ● ●

Monitor Those Voices Continuing with your FBI training, Quy says you should be courageous when you need mental toughness. When she began her training, she had negative thoughts when something new felt uncomfortable. But then she realized that these unhelpful thoughts only lived in her head. She advises you to monitor internal voices that can cause you to doubt yourself and to push them aside before they become powerful.

Gratitude Day Write about a time when you had to persevere and work through a challenge. What was a negative thought you had to ignore? Is it gratifying to look back on your accomplishment now?

_____

_____

_____

_____

_____

_____

_____

_____

• • •

Should or Must Jaime Kulaga says you need to make your self-talk more positive to increase your confidence. Strive to reduce the *should've*, *could've*, and *would've* thoughts, because they fill us with guilt.

(Reminder: tomorrow is Kindness Day.)

Today Which *should've*, *could've*, and *would've* thoughts need to be reduced in your life?

_____

_____

_____

_____

_____

_____

_____

_____

_____

_____

_____

● ● ●

Positive Loop Researchers at Harvard Business School found that kindness and happiness reinforce each other. Participants who had been happiest giving money to others were most likely to give money again during the study. Doubling down on altruism helps make the world a better place.

Today Write about how happy you are with your weekly Kindness Day.

_____

_____

_____

_____

_____

_____

_____

_____

_____

❏ **Kindness Day** Did you do three acts of kindness in the last 24 hours?

• • •

Surmounting Challenges No one can avoid all the challenges and setbacks of life. When a challenge happens to you, don't try to ignore how you feel. Be mindful and look at your emotions. Staying calm in the face of pain, fear, or anger can help you navigate through it and build your resilience. You don't need to revisit a memory, because that triggers stress chemicals in your body, but you can reframe it as indicated below.

Today Picture the anger you once experienced enclosed in a single drop of water, and watch it drop into a pond, making only a small ripple before it's absorbed into calmness. Write about how this makes you feel now.

_____

_____

_____

_____

_____

_____

_____

_____

_____

• • •

Lessen Stress If there's a project you need to have done in a week or two that's causing you a lot of stress, here's how you should do it. Spend two minutes, twice a day, today and tomorrow, calmly visualizing the project completed to your satisfaction. On the third day, you'll have more energy and be ready to tackle the project.

Today What's a project you can apply this to?

_____

_____

_____

_____

_____

_____

_____

_____

_____

_____

_____

_____

● ● ●

Release the Victim Trap Take responsibility for your own thoughts and actions. Follow author Wayne Dyer's advice: when something negative occurs, take a step back before you react and then respond. By doing this, you won't be the victim of your situation but rather a person in charge of their strength and power.

Today Briefly think of a negative trigger person. Imagine how you'll calmly respond instead of reacting the next time you can't avoid them. Describe this.

_____

_____

_____

_____

_____

_____

_____

_____

_____

_____

• • •

Attention Please When you focus your attention on positive things, you begin to notice more and more positive things around you. Author Wayne Dyer said that positive people live in a friendly and loving world while negative people live in a hostile and unfriendly world.

Today Write about something positive you noticed or experienced in the last 24 hours.

_____

_____

_____

_____

_____

_____

_____

_____

_____

_____

_____

_____

• • •

Trust and Listen When you listen to your intuition and trust your heart, you'll be following the best path for your life. A door may be closed, but be persistent; following your dreams will make you stronger and you'll have the life that is best for you.

Gratitude Day Write about a time when you followed your intuition and heart that makes you feel grateful.

_____

_____

_____

_____

_____

_____

_____

_____

_____

_____

● ● ●

Expect Miracles Psychologist Carl Jung coined the term *syn-chronicities*, a term for when events occur with no relationship to each other but seem to be related on a deeper level. These events are also called "meaningful coincidences."

(Reminder: tomorrow is Kindness Day.)

Today Write about a meaningful coincidence you've experienced. Describe how you felt.

_____

_____

_____

_____

_____

_____

_____

_____

_____

_____

• • •

Zoning-Out Permitted Research shows that when people need to do a challenging task, they'd perform better if they first did an easy task that allows the mind to wander. Think of an easy daily task that can help with a more difficult one. Whoever knew laundry or sorting mail was so important?

Today What's your new zoning-out task?

_____

_____

_____

_____

_____

_____

_____

_____

_____

_____

❏ **Kindness Day** Did you do three acts of kindness in the last 24 hours?

• • •

Out of Your Comfort Zone Dr. Kirsten Sanford, creator of
the "This Week in Science" podcast and radio show, explains
in an article on the *Forbes* WomensMedia online channel that
during the Paleolithic era humans lived in small, nomadic
communities, spending their days as hunter-gatherers. Our
brains were "tuned" to this simple, roving existence. She says
that in the modern world, we are faced with different challenges that our brains are not accustomed to. So, with all the
changes that continue to happen in the world, how do we
survive? Dr. Sanford suggests getting out of your comfort
zone and trying something you would not normally do.

Today What can you do in the next 24 hours that's out of your
comfort zone? Start a conversation with a stranger? Or something larger, like asking your boss for a promotion?

_____

_____

_____

_____

_____

_____

_____

• • •

Laugh Out Loud Don't bother putting in extra effort to stifle a laugh. Studies show that people who laugh out loud while watching a funny movie enjoy themselves more than those who try to hide it.

Today What's a funny movie that made you laugh out loud?

_____

_____

_____

_____

_____

_____

_____

_____

_____

_____

_____

_____

● ● ●

You Deserve It You may believe that there are a few people in your life who do not deserve your positive thoughts. You're probably thinking, *Yes, because they're terrible*. They may not deserve them, but you do! You don't need negative and nasty chemicals floating through your body each time you have these thoughts. So let's put a spin on them.

Today Find one little positive thing about each "undeserving" person and write it down. When you think of that person, put this bit of positivity at the front of your mind. You'll be doing yourself a favor!

_____

_____

_____

_____

_____

_____

_____

_____

• • •

Lose Track of Time When you're going through a stressful time, do more of an activity that truly engages you. Have you ever found yourself losing track of time and being totally in the moment? This often happens during an activity that challenges you. Add more of this to your life!

Today What's an activity you could do this week to relieve stress?

_____

_____

_____

_____

_____

_____

_____

_____

_____

_____

• • •

A New Blessing Professor Bryant suggests that each night in bed you should think of a recent blessing that you have yet to be thankful for. By doing this, you'll be savoring the moment, bringing on a positive feeling.

Gratitude Day Taking Bryant's advice, what new blessing will you give thanks for tonight?

_____

_____

_____

_____

_____

_____

_____

_____

_____

_____

_____

_____

● ● ●

More Efficiency Neuroscientist Daniel J. Levitin says our brains have evolved to focus on one task at a time. Today we allow ourselves to be overloaded with information and think the solution is multitasking. The truth is, we're still focusing on one thing at a time; we're just jumping back and forth between tasks, which is much less efficient and much more stressful.

(Reminder: tomorrow is Kindness Day.)

Today Write about something you can do tomorrow where you can focus on one thing at a time. Won't that feel great?

_____

_____

_____

_____

_____

_____

_____

_____

_____

_____

● ● ●

Reducing Stress Our brains have formed to react quickly to threats, releasing stress hormones to alert the fight-or-flight response in our amygdala. When those hormones are released, you're filled with anxiety and stress. One proven way to reduce this situation is with a calm or loving hug. A hug or friendly touch triggers the release of oxytocin, sometimes called the "tend and befriend," hormone which brings the body back to a calm state. It reduces blood pressure and improves your mood.

Today Write about someone who could use a calming, friendly touch when talking with you.

_____

_____

_____

_____

_____

_____

_____

_____

❏ Kindness Day Did you do three acts of kindness in the last 24 hours?

• • •

Don't Be a Killjoy! When you've had a bad day, try not to focus on negative things that have occurred. People who savor the positive instead of the negative of every situation are happier at the end of the day.

Today Write about the most positive thing that happened today. How does this make you feel? You're building up your positivity. Doesn't that fact alone make you feel great?

_____

_____

_____

_____

_____

_____

_____

_____

_____

_____

_____

● ● ●

Time Flies A good way to increase your positivity is to remember that time flies. This will remind you to be in the moment and to enjoy all the good that is happening around you.

Today Since you know how time flies, write about the best thing that happened this month and remind yourself to savor it and re-create it in your mind. Doing this will help you become a more positive person.

_____

_____

_____

_____

_____

_____

_____

_____

_____

_____

_____

● ● ●

Permission to Compare Professor Bryant says that one way to boost positive feelings is to remind yourself that things could be worse. For example, if you're having a stressful day at work, remind yourself of people who may not have a job at all. Comparing your experience with a worse one gives you a point of reference and makes you feel a little better.

Today Compare something great in your life with how you'd feel if you didn't have it. Try to put a positive spin on that.

_____

_____

_____

_____

_____

_____

_____

_____

_____

_____

● ● ●

Real to the Brain Visualizing a success activates the same parts of your brain as if you were actually experiencing that accomplishment. Research shows that it increases your positivity.

Today What personal success do you hope will happen in the next week? Now visualize and write about it in detail. Experience it with emotion, as if it's happening right now.

_____

_____

_____

_____

_____

_____

_____

_____

_____

_____

_____

• • •

To Compare or Not to Compare, That Is the Question We've discussed how ads encourage you to compare yourself with others by evoking feelings of envy or jealousy. Instead of comparing yourself to others, the better tip is to compare your new improved self with how you used to be.

Gratitude Day Write about how you've improved in one area of your life over the last 10 years. Isn't it gratifying to make this type of comparison?

_____

_____

_____

_____

_____

_____

_____

_____

_____

_____

• • •

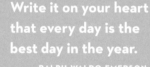

Write it on your heart
that every day is the
best day in the year.

RALPH WALDO EMERSON,
Society and Solitude (1870)

Degrees of Love One form of love is having a positive conversation with someone that makes you feel connected and in tune with them. All forms of love have health benefits that you can enjoy.

(Reminder: tomorrow is Kindness Day.)

Today In the last 24 hours, what were the three longest interpersonal interactions you had? How connected did you feel?

_____

_____

_____

_____

_____

_____

_____

_____

_____

_____

• • •

Connect with Gratitude A study led by Nathaniel Lambert, a social psychology expert, found that when we express gratitude to our significant other or to a close friend, it helps to strengthen those relationships.

Today Write about which close friend you'll express gratitude to next. What will you say?

_____

_____

_____

_____

_____

_____

_____

_____

_____

_____

❏ Kindness Day Did you do three acts of kindness in the last 24 hours?

• • •

Gestures Reveal Communications expert Dianna Booher says that particular gestures reveal signs of stress. Some signs are tapping your fingers or your feet, twirling your necklace or twisting your ring, rubbing your neck, and crossing your arms.

Today Write about a time when you thought you'd be very nervous but instead spoke and performed very well.

_____

_____

_____

_____

_____

_____

_____

_____

_____

_____

_____

• • •

More than Hearing Booher says that listening helps you become a strong communicator in several ways. When you genuinely listen to a conversation, you are giving your attention to the other person, you learn something new, and you can respond appropriately.

Today Who will you be speaking with soon so that you can practice truly listening?

_____

_____

_____

_____

_____

_____

_____

_____

_____

_____

_____

● ● ●

This Takes Practice When someone is telling you about a situation that caused them great positive emotion, don't try to tell them about a similar situation you experienced. It turns the focus off of them and on to you. This one takes practice!

Today Write about a time when someone told you about something that made them very happy. Describe what you'll say the next time you see this person to remind them of that happy time. Both of you will feel better for it.

_____ _____

_____ _____

_____

_____

_____

_____

_____

_____

_____

_____

● ○ ●

Please Allow Venting There are times when a friend needs to vent, elaborate, and vent some more. Mark Goulston, author of *Just Listen,* says that instead of jumping in and trying to solve their problem for them or sitting in silence, there are three questions you should ask them. These questions will help you understand what they're frustrated, angry, and worried about. First ask them "What is making you frustrated?" Then allow them to vent. If they tell you that they made a mistake, ask them to go into more detail so they get all of their frustrations out.

Today Write about a time when you vented to a friend and then realized you felt immensely better.

_____

_____

_____

_____

_____

_____

_____

_____

_____

● ● ●

Emotional Drain Overflow The second question you should ask your friend when they are venting is "What is upsetting you the most?" Since you are dealing with an outpouring of negative emotions, I would suggest using Goulston's advice for self-protection. He says to let whatever they are venting about to roll off you so that it does not affect you.

Gratitude Day List three things you've been grateful for in the last week.

_____

_____

_____

_____

_____

_____

_____

_____

_____

_____

• • •

Date _____   **Week 42** • **Day 6**

Bottom-Out the Venting The last question you can ask when someone is venting is "What is really concerning you?" Once you hear the main reason behind their worry, reassure them that you understand their concerns and try to come up with solutions together to help them. Acting as your executive coach, I'd say most people find their own best solution. Hold back on your perfect solution and see what arises from them. Your solution might be out of their capability zone.

(Reminder: tomorrow is Kindness Day.)

Today Write about a time when you had a perfect solution for a friend and they chose to do something different. Will you try to hold back next time? Isn't it relaxing to realize you aren't going to try to solve their problems?

_____

_____

_____

_____

_____

_____

_____

_____

● ● ●

Kindness Question of the Day Researchers in Great Britain have found that doing a good deed each day makes people happier in as little as 10 days. So ask yourself, "Did I make someone feel good today?"

Today Write about some kind things you could do today.

_____

_____

_____

_____

_____

_____

_____

_____

_____

_____

❏ **Kindness Day** Did you do three acts of kindness in the last 24 hours?

● ● ●

Feeling Good All the Time Does it help you to be happier if you avoid negative things? Researchers have found that the happiest people don't ignore the negative, but rather focus on the positive when things go wrong. Our brains are on alert with a negativity bias, so we have to work a little harder to notice the positive, but it's definitely worth doing!

Today Write about something positive that happened this week that you'd enjoy savoring a little bit longer.

_____

_____

_____

_____

_____

_____

_____

_____

_____

• • •

Question the Negative You know you shouldn't ignore the negative—including those persistent negative thoughts. What *should* you do? Let's question one negative view or judgment about yourself with advice from Dr. Hanson. He says to answer these questions: "Am I really sure? What else could be true? How does this make me feel? Am I getting attached to my views rather than holding them lightly?"

Today Write about one familiar thought and the answers to these four questions.

_____

_____

_____

_____

_____

_____

_____

_____

_____

_____

• • •

Hard to Handle Have you ever had to deal with a difficult person? Do you still talk to a difficult person? A good idea is to reflect things back to them. If they are giving you a hard time, you can say, "Does that sound fair?" It'll give you a little more time to think of how to change the direction of the conversation, and hopefully it will steer them to self-reflect.

Today Write about a question you can use for those hard-to-handle people.

_____

_____

_____

_____

_____

_____

_____

_____

_____

_____

● ● ●

Challenging Comfort Great things can happen when you take a step out of your comfort zone. What if you made a commitment to say "yes" to every opportunity that came your way for a specific period of time? Think of how this could expand your life.

Today What opportunities are you turning down that can change your life? Will you say "yes" for one week or one month? Make an open announcement to others.

_____

_____

_____

_____

_____

_____

_____

_____

_____

_____

● ● ●

Surprise! I agree with author Christine Carter, who says you shouldn't buy gifts from a registry. She explains that the reason we love presents so much is because we love the excitement of discovering what's inside. So don't give them that blender on their list. Think of a surprise gift you can give someone this week. It doesn't have to be anything big—it'll let them know you're thinking of them.

Gratitude Day List three things you're grateful for this week.

_____

_____

_____

_____

_____

_____

_____

_____

_____

_____

• • •

Satisfice Means Less Stress Nobel Laureate Herbert Simon coined the word "satisfice" to mean picking an option within reasonable limits instead of aiming for perfection. When people decide to aim for results that are good enough, they experience less stress. Studies show that, of people aiming for perfection, the maximizers suffered more stress, less life satisfaction, and more self-criticism about their decisions. The satisficers were pleased that they made the first choice that met their criteria; they weren't seeking perfection.

(Reminder: tomorrow is Kindness Day.)

Today In what area of your life do you think being a satisficer would be an improvement?

_____

_____

_____

_____

_____

_____

_____

_____

_____

● ● ●

Kindness Day Money isn't the only thing you can donate. You can also volunteer your talents and reap the same benefits. It's not only beneficial for the recipient but for your health and happiness as well as for the community.

Today Write about an instance when you volunteered your talents. Did you feel happier?

_____

_____

_____

_____

_____

_____

_____

_____

_____

❏ Kindness Day Did you do three acts of kindness in the last 24 hours?

● ● ●

Win a New Friend Is there someone you'd like to go out with? The first step is to ask them, although your inner negative voice may be telling you that they are too busy. Invite them to meet for coffee or lunch.

Today Write about the person you'd like to go out with. What topic could bring you together?

_____

_____

_____

_____

_____

_____

_____

_____

_____

_____

_____

_____

• • •

Eye to Eye Have you ever been talking to someone and noticed their eyes shifting around rather than looking directly at you? Don't let this happen when you're talking. Look directly into a person's eyes and hold it for two to three seconds before looking away.

Today Who do you know who's good with this eye skill? You can train yourself to learn this skill.

_____

_____

_____

_____

_____

_____

_____

_____

_____

_____

• • •

Hi-Bye Friends Life coach Celestine Chua says that when you want to expand the number of friends you do things with, you should reach out to your hi-bye friends. These are the friends you see in school or at work—you greet each other at the beginning and end of the day and that's about it. Drop them a friendly message and see if there's an opportunity to reconnect.

Today Who's a hi-bye friend you'd like to develop into a true friend?

_____

_____

_____

_____

_____

_____

_____

_____

_____

_____

● ● ●

222

Friendship Containers Shasta Nelson, author of *Friendships Don't Just Happen!,* says that for good friendships to form, you need consistency. She recommends joining groups, such as book clubs, elective courses, or workshops. She calls these groups "friendship containers." When you join a group, the consistency is built in because there is a scheduled time to show up.

Today Write about a new friendship container you could look into. If you already have one, write about how good it makes you feel.

• • •

Don't Stay Trapped in the Container Keep in mind that the goal of the friendship container is to give you the connection and ability to move beyond it. You can initiate meetings, coffee, dinners, or even vacations. The idea is to entwine your lives together in more than one way.

Gratitude Day Write about one friendship that expanded beyond the friendship container. For even more gratitude, list four other friends you're grateful to have.

_____

_____

_____

_____

_____

_____

_____

_____

_____

_____

● ● ●

Deep Friendship Requires Vulnerability There are three aspects to friendships that are nonnegotiable: positivity, consistency, and vulnerability. If any of these are missing, it will create an obstacle. If you have only positivity and consistency, it means you're going out and having a good time, but you're not feeling known. Shasta Nelson says that vulnerability helps us feel safe and connected. For deeper friendships, you need to have people who know what's going on in your daily life. You have to be open and let them know your struggles and vice versa. Social media is great for initiating contacts, but deepening them is up to you.

(Reminder: tomorrow is Kindness Day.)

Today Write about one of your social media contacts that you'd like to grow into a deeper friendship. What can you arrange?

_____

_____

_____

_____

_____

_____

_____

● ● ●

Friends' Friends Celestine Chua recommends you get to know your friends' friends. You can join them in their outings or ask your friend to introduce you. If you're comfortable with your friends, there's a good chance you'll be comfortable with their friends.

Today Which friend do you think is a good friends' friend connection for you?

_____

_____

_____

_____

_____

_____

_____

_____

_____

❏ **Kindness Day** Did you do three acts of kindness in the last 24 hours?

● ● ●

Jumping Out of Your Comfort Zone What's one thing you'd like to accomplish this year that is outside your comfort zone? Therapist Sherry Collier advises you to recognize your negative thoughts on this subject and replace them with positive thoughts. Take a negative what-if thought, like "What if I fail?" and replace it with a positive possibility, like "What if it turns out even better than I expected?"

Today Write about one thing you'd like to accomplish this year that's outside your comfort zone.

_____

_____

_____

_____

_____

_____

_____

_____

_____

_____

• • •

Take Adventurous Action Against Your Fear Use your fears
to challenge yourself to new summits. The best antidote to fear
is action. Take an adventurous approach to something you
fear. The crazy thing about fear is that it's an emotion that's
rarely based on truth. Don't let a distorted version of reality
stop you from making gains.

Today Don't take an ordinary step here. What's an adventurous step you can take to launch yourself toward one thing you
want to accomplish this year?

_____

_____

_____

_____

_____

_____

_____

_____

● ● ●

Can I Savor Procrastination? Author Leo Babauta says that we procrastinate because we're uncomfortable with a task and want to do something easier and more familiar instead. If there's a project you need to tackle, savor it. Notice your urge to take a look at something else, but don't do it. There's usually an enjoyable aspect in every activity.

Today Write about a task that you're uncomfortable doing this week. What could be an enjoyable aspect of it?

_____

_____

_____

_____

_____

_____

_____

_____

• • •

Dispute a Worry Unnecessary negative thoughts give rise to negative emotions, feed on each other, and start a downward spiral. One proven technique that works is to dispute these thoughts. Talk to yourself as if you're talking to a good friend. Say, "What's going on here? Aren't you magnifying things out of proportion? Let's check the facts."

Today Apply this to something you're worrying about this week.

_____

_____

_____

_____

_____

_____

_____

_____

_____

_____

• • •

The Worry Cycle Sometimes you may find yourself starting an endless cycle of worrying about things that you aren't changing. The first step is to acknowledge this cycle, and the second step is to find a healthy distraction. Go out in nature, exercise, listen to uplifting music, or visit a friend. Think about a nature distraction you've enjoyed in the past. Take a minute, savor it, and feel grateful.

Gratitude Day What are three things that happened this week that you're grateful for?

_____

_____

_____

_____

_____

_____

_____

_____

_____

_____

● ● ●

Worried About How You Look and Sound? When you're worrying about how you're coming across to other people, it causes you to stumble and not be perceived as self-confident. So instead, when you find yourself in this position, focus on the other person—be interested in them, ask questions. Make them feel that they're the most important person in the room.

(Reminder: tomorrow is Kindness Day.)

Today What situations make you feel this way? Describe how you can turn that around next time by using this idea.

_____

_____

_____

_____

_____

_____

_____

_____

_____

● ● ●

Is Kindness Contagious? When you truly help someone else, it makes you feel good and also encourages you to keep it up.

Today Which weekly exercise is helping you the most: Gratitude Day or Kindness Day? Or are they both helping you become happier and more fulfilled?

_____

_____

_____

_____

_____

_____

_____

_____

_____

_____

❏ **Kindness Day** Did you do three acts of kindness in the last 24 hours??

• • •

Have a Good Habit? Researchers at Duke have found that approximately 40 percent of our daily activities are habits we've learned.

Today It's time for self-admiration. Write about one good habit you've instilled in your morning routine.

_____

_____

_____

_____

_____

_____

_____

_____

_____

_____

_____

• • •

Building a New Habit James Clear, author of *Transform Your Habits*, has good advice on how to build a new habit. First, decide what's the smallest step you could take toward a new habit. Rather than starting with 50 sit-ups per day, start with five sit-ups. Instead of trying to meditate for 10 minutes each day, start by meditating for one minute each day.

Today Write about a new habit you'd like to start right away.

_____

_____

_____

_____

_____

_____

_____

_____

_____

_____

_____

• • •

Habit Lapse Plan ahead for how you're going to handle when you slip up on your new habit. Emma Seppälä says you should go easy on yourself. Studies show that doing so will help you stay on track the next time and it's much better than criticizing yourself. The important thing here is to see why and how you lose control.

Today Write about a few typical things that can distract you from your new habit and how you plan to handle them.

_____

_____

_____

_____

_____

_____

_____

_____

_____

_____

● ● ●

Of Ultimate Importance for a New Habit James Clear explains that research has shown that missing your habit one time does not impact long-term progress. Everyone gets off track once in a while. The key is to get back on as quickly as possible. You may slip up one day every now and then, but never two days in a row.

Today Write about how you plan to keep track of the new habit you're forming. Do you want to print a calendar page and keep track that way, or maybe have it as a phone or computer reminder?

_____

_____

_____

_____

_____

_____

_____

_____

● ● ●

How's Your 40 Percent Looking? Since 40 percent of your daily activities are habits, picture your best habits and visualize them in full color.

Gratitude Day Write about your top three good habits and how grateful you feel. Give yourself a little pep talk for building a new habit, because tomorrow I'm going to give you a simple way to implement it.

_____

_____

_____

_____

_____

_____

_____

_____

_____

_____

● ● ●

Even 1 Percent Adds Up Take author James Clear's advice and plan on increasing your new good habit by 1 percent a day. Start small and gradually improve. Along the way, your willpower and motivation will increase, which will make it easier to stick to your habit.

(Reminder: tomorrow is Kindness Day.)

Today Picture yourself one year from today performing your habit step-by-step. What do you see, and how does this make you feel?

_____

_____

_____

_____

_____

_____

_____

_____

_____

_____

● ● ●

Segmenting Is Next If you continue adding 1 percent each day, you'll find yourself increasing very quickly within a couple of months. It's important to keep each habit attainable so you can keep improving.

Today Write in detail about the kind act you've done in the last month that you're most proud of, and also add it to your Kindness Treasures page at the end of the journal.

_____

_____

_____

_____

_____

_____

_____

_____

_____

❏ **Kindness Day** Did you do three acts of kindness in the last 24 hours?

● ● ●

Reducing Habit Anxiety You can visualize yourself with a new habit firmly in place, but be sure to include the necessary steps. UCLA researchers found that picturing yourself going through the steps and seeing the new you is much more effective than merely visualizing the finished product. Envisioning the steps has an added benefit of reducing anxiety, because you're imaging how you you'll achieve your new habit.

Today Do this visualization now for a new habit, include steps, and write about how you feel.

_____

_____

_____

_____

_____

_____

_____

_____

_____

_____

• • •

Using Habit Triggers The if-then process works well for establishing a new habit. The idea is to select a task in your daily routine, and once it's completed, you add another one. For instance, "If I sit down at my desk, then I'm going to do one task that makes me happy before I open my e-mail."

Today Write about an if-then you'll add to your daily routine that will make you happy.

_____

_____

_____

_____

_____

_____

_____

_____

_____

_____

• • •

Easy Morning Habit Therapist Marlu Harris suggests easy new habits that will make you happier—one in the morning and one in the evening. In the morning, go outside and look up at the sky. Notice how your body feels with your head tilted up. Take note of the colors in the sky. What sounds do you hear? Do you hear birds or traffic? And for a moment close your eyes, inhale deeply, and exhale. Congratulations: that's a form of meditation.

Today Write about a time when you paid attention to birds singing. Where were you? How did it make you feel?

_____

_____

_____

_____

_____

_____

_____

_____

• • •

Easy Evening Habit Harris has an evening habit that works well, too. Before bedtime, lie down on your back with your arms to your sides with your palms facing up. Take a deep breath and recall something that made you happy, no matter how small it may seem. Now, deeply inhale the gratitude and exhale any negative thoughts or aches and pains you might feel. Take at least three very deep breaths, in through your nose and out through your mouth.

Today Practice this habit now, and afterward write about the happy event you recalled.

_____

_____

_____

_____

_____

_____

_____

_____

_____

• • •

A Different Take on Gratitude Instead of looking around at things that make you grateful, it's also important to appreciate your responses to people and situations. Sometimes there are difficult people you cannot avoid and situations that are out of your control, which cause automatic negative reactions from you. If you see the trigger starting, you can decide to modify or reduce your reaction. You should appreciate this positive control you're displaying.

Gratitude Day Write about three people or situations that act as negative triggers for you, and how you plan to change your reactions. You can be grateful for these intentions and for the positive pathways you'll be forging in your brain.

_____

_____

_____

_____

_____

_____

_____

• • •

Five Years Ago Compare yourself today to how you were five years ago. Have you made progress on your personal goals?

(Reminder: tomorrow is Kindness Day.)

Today Write about one goal you achieved in the last five years.

_____

_____

_____

_____

_____

_____

_____

_____

_____

_____

_____

_____

• • •

Have a Savor Habit The new habit you're developing is going to make you a better person. To strengthen your habit, take a few moments to pay attention, and savor what you're doing. For example, author Leo Babauta says that when you're exercising, pay attention to the movement of your body, feel the effort of each move, your breathing, and your concentration. The goal isn't the accomplishment, but the journey it takes to get there.

Today Write about how you can apply this to your new habit.

_____

_____

_____

_____

_____

_____

_____

_____

_____

❏ **Kindness Day** Did you do three acts of kindness in the last 24 hours?

● ● ●

Good Stress Many people believe reducing stress is the key to happiness. However, Michelle McQuaid, author of *Your Strengths Blueprint*, mentions that the Gallup World Happiness Report found that countries with a high level of stress also had a high level of happiness. People who live happily are not necessarily free from stress, and living a stress-free life doesn't automatically promise happiness.

Today How is stress helping you in your life? Does it help you aspire to new achievements?

_____

_____

_____

_____

_____

_____

_____

_____

_____

_____

• • •

Flourishing Researchers have found that both positive and negative emotions have their place when it comes to flourishing. Positive emotions can boost your energy, self-confidence, and creativity. Negative emotions can trigger your awareness that something important to you is not right.

Today Is there something you're currently sensing is not right? Keeping this on a positive note, aren't you glad your emotions sent you a nudge? Write about this.

_____

_____

_____

_____

_____

_____

_____

_____

_____

_____

• • •

Invest in Yourself Sherry Collier says to invest money in your personal development. When times are tight, our first reaction is to cut back on self-development. Instead of cutting back, find some interesting ways to invest in yourself. This will signal to your own psyche that you value yourself and have faith to grow.

Today Write about three things you can do to add to your self-development.

_____

_____

_____

_____

_____

_____

_____

_____

_____

_____

• • •

Not Easy When you want to achieve something that's in line with your skills, for it to be truly satisfying, it can't be easy for you—otherwise it will be boring. When you find that challenge and take it head-on, you'll find it rewarding.

Today Write about one challenge you enjoy taking.

_____

_____

_____

_____

_____

_____

_____

_____

_____

_____

_____

_____

• • •

Meaning and Purpose Professor Adam Grant says that we feel a sense of purpose in our lives when we have the belief that what we do or contribute has a positive impact on others.

Gratitude Day Write about something you do that has a positive impact on others. Make yourself a little happier and grateful right now by savoring this.

_____

_____

_____

_____

_____

_____

_____

_____

_____

_____

_____

• • •

More Meaning To find more meaning in your life, take a look at your relationships. It's important to see other people's problems and reassure them in their ability to handle them. (Notice that I didn't say solve their problems for them.) Helping people this way gives your life more meaning and purpose.

(Reminder: tomorrow is Kindness Day.)

Today Write about who could benefit from your assurance in their ability to handle current problems.

_____

_____

_____

_____

_____

_____

_____

_____

_____

_____

• • •

Each Kind Act Matters Professor Lyubomirsky was the first to show evidence that doing acts of kindness increases a person's contentment. One main reason is because it gives a person a sense of purpose. Each small act makes the world a little better.

Today Write about one thing that gives you this feeling.

_____

_____

_____

_____

_____

_____

_____

_____

_____

_____

❏ **Kindness Day** Did you do three acts of kindness in the last 24 hours?

● ● ●

Encouraging Others People don't usually take into consideration how much knowledge you have until they see how much effort you show. Ask questions and take a sincere interest in others.

Today Write about someone you know who could use your encouragement.

_____

_____

_____

_____

_____

_____

_____

_____

_____

_____

_____

_____

_____

• • •

Experience Encourages Others Michael Angier, author of
The Achievement Code, says to share from your own experience.
You have much more to share than you realize. You may be
the only one who can touch someone with your inspiring
experience.

Today What is one of your positive experiences that you
believe would encourage someone else?

_____

_____

_____

_____

_____

_____

_____

_____

_____

_____

● ● ●

Date _____   **Week 49** ● **Day 3**

Even Vulnerability Can Encourage Others It's important to share your challenges and failures as well as your successes with others. It encourages them to push forward.

Today Write about one of your challenges and whether you can improve things with a new habit.

_____

_____

_____

_____

_____

_____

_____

_____

_____

_____

_____

_____

● ● ●

Date _____   **Week 49 • Day 4**

Practice Carefrontation Author Michael Angier says that when we challenge people, we push them to be the best version of themselves. Many of us have had a teacher who challenged us to do our best, and we became better for it. Practice "carefrontation," which is carefully and caringly challenging others.

Today Write about a time when you used "carefrontation." Are you better for this experience?

_____

_____

_____

_____

_____

_____

_____

_____

_____

_____

_____

• • •

Encourage Others with Books Read, stay informed, and share what you read with others. Tell people about books that have inspired you. Share the knowledge.

Gratitude Day Write about three books you're grateful to have read.

_____

_____

_____

_____

_____

_____

_____

_____

_____

_____

_____

_____

• • •

Encourage Others with Communication Learning to communicate effectively is a critical element to inspire others. Watch how you speak and what you say. Invest in your communication skills. Have you thought about increasing your communication skills?

(Reminder: tomorrow is Kindness Day.)

Today Write about a person you know who has great communication skills.

_____

_____

_____

_____

_____

_____

_____

_____

_____

_____

● ● ●

Awe and Kindness An excellent way to tap into feelings of compassion and concern for others is to take an "awe walk." This requires going for a walk somewhere that seems boundless and helps you feel connected to what's around you. Researcher Paul Piff did a study where half the participants stood in a field of eucalyptus trees and looked up for just a minute; the other participants looked away from the trees, at a building. Afterward the tree gazers were more likely to help someone in need and less likely to feel that they were superior to others.

Today It may not have been in a field of eucalyptus trees, but where have you experienced awe such as this?

_____

_____

_____

_____

_____

_____

❏ Kindness Day Did you do three acts of kindness in the last 24 hours?

● ● ●

Assign to Autopilot According to Robert Pozen, lecturer at the MIT Sloan School of Management, if you want to maintain long-term discipline, it's best to identify the things in your life that you consider mundane and keep those aspects consistent. Let these tasks run on autopilot while you save your energy for decisions that are more important. A double benefit is that your creative right brain can take over during these subconscious routines.

Today What's one routine you can assign to autopilot?

_____

_____

_____

_____

_____

_____

_____

_____

_____

_____

• • •

Ruin Rumination The happiest people try to avoid overthinking. Susan Nolen-Hoeksema, author of *Women Who Think Too Much*, said that people often think that overthinking is going to help the situation, but it often makes it worse.

Today When do you find yourself overthinking? What's a distraction or activity you can use to interrupt overthinking?

_____

_____

_____

_____

_____

_____

_____

_____

_____

_____

● ● ●

Smile or Laugh Author Christine Carter says that when we crack a smile—a genuine eye crinkle that researchers call a "Duchenne smile"—our cardiovascular system calms. Laughing takes it one step further, partly because it forces us to exhale. Simply exhaling lowers our heart rate and induces feelings of calm.

Today Write about something that recently made you laugh out loud.

_____

_____

_____

_____

_____

_____

_____

_____

_____

_____

• • •

Have You Read That? Reading exposes you to new ideas, information, and fresh ways of thinking. You'll never run out of things to talk about with new or old acquaintances, because you can always revert to something you've read.

Today Write about what you've read recently that you found interesting or entertaining.

_____

_____

_____

_____

_____

_____

_____

_____

_____

_____

_____

● ● ●

Surprise! Things that are unexpected cause stronger feelings of gratitude.

Gratitude Day Write in detail about one surprising thing that you're grateful for. Take a minute to savor it.

_____

_____

_____

_____

_____

_____

_____

_____

_____

_____

_____

_____

● ● ●

Praising Others Professor Kenna Griffin has good advice about acknowledging the good that others are doing. She says you shouldn't hesitate to praise someone's efforts and, if you can, address their great job publicly as well.

(Reminder: tomorrow is Kindness Day.)

Today Who is someone who's doing a good job and would benefit from a high-five from you?

_____

_____

_____

_____

_____

_____

_____

_____

_____

_____

_____

_____

• • •

Grow Your Optimism Studies at the Greater Good Science
Center at UC Berkeley show that practicing gratitude increases
your level of optimism. Now, if you're a pessimistic person,
you might've thought that wasn't possible!

Today Write with an optimistic view about something that's
coming up in your life. What's a step you can take to help this
happen?

_____

_____

_____

_____

_____

_____

_____

_____

_____

❏ Kindness Day Did you do three acts of kindness in the last
24 hours?

• • •

Your Happiness Backpack Happiness is composed of multiple elements, such as positive emotions, relationships, a sense of meaning and accomplishment, and good physical health.

Today Looking over the past week, what situation brought you the most happiness? Did it involve more than one of the above elements?

_____

_____

_____

_____

_____

_____

_____

_____

_____

_____

_____

● ● ●

Increase the Positive We need positive emotions in our life. At the beginning of this year, we worked through the ten positive emotions as outlined by Professor Fredrickson: joy, gratitude, serenity, interest, hope, pride, amusement, inspiration, awe, and love.

Today Write about one of these positive emotions that you experienced this week.

_____

_____

_____

_____

_____

_____

_____

_____

_____

_____

_____

● ● ●

Enjoying Engagement When you're fully engaged in a task or situation that's not easy, you experience being in the flow. This mean you concentrate intensely on the present and may even lose your sense of time. This feels good and contributes to your well-being.

Today Write about one situation or project in the last month that fully engaged you.

_____

_____

_____

_____

_____

_____

_____

_____

_____

_____

_____

● ● ●

People People As humans, we are social beings, and the positive and meaningful relationships we have contribute to our happiness.

Today Write about a person you can turn to for support during difficult times.

_____

_____

_____

_____

_____

_____

_____

_____

_____

_____

_____

_____

• • •

Nonmaterial Meaning Rather than following the pursuit of possessions and wealth, you need to find a greater purpose in life. When you focus on kindness, you experience a cause bigger than yourself.

Gratitude Day Write about one time when you felt this because you performed a kind act. Include how grateful you were because you extended yourself in this manner.

_____

_____

_____

_____

_____

_____

_____

_____

_____

_____

_____

● ● ●

Aspire and Accomplish Having real goals and ambitions to achieve things gives you a sense of accomplishment. When you succeed with steps toward your goals, you feel a sense of pride and fulfillment.

(Reminder: tomorrow is Kindness Day.)

Today Write about one accomplishment you're proud of.

_____

_____

_____

_____

_____

_____

_____

_____

_____

_____

_____

● ● ●

Kindness with Benefits Doing a kind act without expecting anything in return is what we've been working toward. Guess what? The other person benefits, as do you. Research has shown that kind people live longer and healthier lives. When you're helping another person you get the "helper's high" feeling that's associated with lowered anxiety and depression. Another benefit is that the other person and any observers may have a pay-it-forward urge that will continue the kindness cycle.

Today Write about one pay-it-forward kind act you experienced or observed.

_____

_____

_____

_____

_____

_____

_____

❑ **Kindness Day** Did you do three acts of kindness in the last 24 hours?

● ● ●

Pleasure and Meaning Psychology professor Tal Ben-Shahar taught one of the most popular classes at Harvard. It was a course on positive psychology in which he taught the class how to be happy. He says happiness lies at the intersection between pleasure and meaning. Whether at work or at home, the goal is to engage in activities that are both personally significant and enjoyable. When this is not possible, make sure you have happiness boosters, such as moments throughout the week that give you both pleasure and meaning. Research shows that an hour or two of a meaningful and pleasurable experience can affect the quality of an entire day or even a whole week.

Today Write about something that has both pleasure and meaning for you. Be sure to draw a star next to it!

_____

_____

_____

_____

_____

_____

_____

_____

● ● ●

Cherish Your Choices You can make choices or merely let life happen to you. I'm sure you can think of someone who went through life stagnant. You're different. Make a decision that honors your values and aspirations and then here's what you do next: congratulate yourself on what a good decision this is and how great you feel taking charge of your life.

Today Write about a recent decision and congratulate yourself on not living a passive life!

_____

_____

_____

_____

_____

_____

_____

_____

_____

_____

● ● ●

Daily Dose of Dopamine Wouldn't you like a little bit of the happy-brain chemical dopamine every day? Celebrating small steps triggers more dopamine than saving it up waiting for one big achievement. It's free, it has no calories, and it doesn't impair your driving. You have small victories every day. Why not enjoy them?

Today Write about a small positive step you've taken in the last 24 hours. Savor the feeling of a happy brain.

_____

_____

_____

_____

_____

_____

_____

_____

_____

_____

● ● ●

Chemistry 101 Professor Fredrickson says there's a subtle flow of the happy-brain chemical oxytocin during everyday activities like talking with friends, playing with your kids, or closing a deal at work. Or you can do something for yourself, like getting a massage.

Today Write about the ways you plan to get those subtle doses of oxytocin this week.

_____

_____

_____

_____

_____

_____

_____

_____

_____

_____

_____

• • •

Gratitude Benefits You You've been encouraged to pay more attention to being grateful over these last 12 months. Professor Robert Emmons' research shows that this benefits you physically with a stronger immune system and fewer aches and pains. It helps you psychologically by giving you more joy, optimism, happiness, and pleasure. Socially, it helps you become less lonely, more helpful, compassionate, and more forgiving.

Gratitude Day Today, write about one of these areas where you've seen how gratitude has helped you.

_____

_____

_____

_____

_____

_____

_____

_____

_____

_____

• • •

At the End of the Day Ask yourself these questions at the end of the day:

Did I feel grateful for something?

Was I kind to someone, or was someone kind to me?

Did I do something that brought me happiness?

Can I see value in something I did?

Today Write about one of these questions that you answered with a *yes*.

_____

_____

_____

_____

_____

_____

_____

_____

_____

_____

_____

● ● ●

Year-End Reward You've been practicing kindness and gratitude for a year now. You've taken the 40 percent of your happiness that is under your control and worked with it! When you look around, do you see people who haven't even begun this journey? They probably believe their situations prevent them from improving. Help them see that five minutes a day can deliver a happier and more fulfilling life. Pass your good work forward!

Today Write yourself a heartfelt thank-you for working on your 40 percent.

_____

_____

_____

_____

_____

_____

_____

_____

_____

● ● ●

KINDNESS TREASURES

List the kind acts you're most proud of. Thank you for helping make the world a better place.

_____

_____

_____

_____

_____

_____

_____

_____

_____

_____

_____

_____

_____

_____

_____

● ● ●

CONTRIBUTORS

Shawn Achor is a researcher at Harvard University, the founder of GoodThinkInc., the chief experience officer at BetterUp, and the author of *The Happiness Advantage*.

Michael E. Angier is the founder of SuccessNet and the author of *The Achievement Code: The Three-C Formula for Getting What You Truly Want*.

Leo Babauta is the founder of Zen Habits Radio and is the author of *The Power of Less: The Fine Art of Limiting Yourself to the Essential . . . in Business and in Life*.

Joshua Becker is the founder of Becoming Minimalist and is the author of *The More of Less: Finding the Life You Want Under Everything You Own*.

Tal Ben-Shahar is an expert in leadership development and cofounder of Potentialife. He is the author of *Happier: Learn the Secrets to Daily Joy and Lasting Fulfillment*.

Dianna Booher is CEO of the Booher Research Institute and author of *What More Can I Say?: Why Communication Fails and What to Do About It*.

Fred B. Bryant is a professor of psychology at Loyola University Chicago and the coauthor of *Savoring: A New Model of Positive Experience*.

Brad Bushman is a professor of communication and psychology and Margaret Hall and Robert Randal Rinehart Chair of Mass Communication at The Ohio State University.

Olivia Fox Cabane is an expert in the fields of charisma and leadership, author of *The Charisma Myth: How Anyone Can Master the Art and Science of Personal Magnetism*, and coauthor of *The Net and the Butterfly: The Art and Practice of Breakthrough Thinking*.

Christine Carter is a sociologist and senior fellow at University of California, Berkeley's Greater Good Science Center and the author of *The Sweet Spot: How to Find Your Groove at Home and Work*.

Erica Chadwick is a clinical psychologist and founding director of mindbranch in New Zealand.

Celestine Chua is a life coach and founder of the *Personal Excellence* podcast and blog.

James Clear writes about science-based ideas for living a better life and is the author of *Transform Your Habits*.

Sherry Collier is a therapist and business consultant.

Mihaly Csikszentmihalyi is Distinguished Professor of Psychology and Management and founder and codirector of the Quality of Life Research Center at Claremont Graduate University. He is also the author of *Flow: The Psychology of Optimal Experience*.

Kevin Daum is on the faculty of Fordham University and is the author of *Roar!: Get Heard in the Sales and Marketing Jungle: A Business Fable*.

Dani DiPirro is the founder of Positively Present and author of *The Positively Present Guide to Life: How to Make the Most of Every Moment*.

harles Duhigg is a senior editor at *The New York Times* and the author of *Smarter Faster Better: The Transformative Power of Real Productivity*.

abeth Dunn is a professor of psychology at the University of British Columbia and the coauthor of *Happy Money: The Science of Happier pending*.

Wayne W. Dyer was an expert in the field of self-development and the author of *The Power of Intention*.

Robert A. Emmons is a professor of psychology at the University of California, Davis, director of the Emmons Lab, and author of *The Little Book of Gratitude: Creating a Life of Happiness and Wellbeing by Giving Thanks*.

Barbara Fredrickson is Director of the Positive Emotions and Psychophysiology Laboratory at the University of North Carolina at Chapel Hill and the author of *Positivity: Top-Notch Research Reveals the Upward Spiral That Will Change Your Life*.

Michael Gervais is a performance psychologist and founder of Finding Mastery.

John Gottman is the cofounder of the Gottman Institute and a renowned relationship researcher and psychologist.

Mark Goulston is a psychiatrist and business coach and the author of *Just Listen: Discover the Secret to Getting Through to Absolutely Anyone*.

Adam Grant is the Saul P. Steinberg Professor of Management at the Wharton School of the University of Pennsylvania and author of *Give and Take: Why Helping Others Drives Our Success* and *Originals: How Non-Conformists Move the World*.

Loretta Graziano Breuning is the founder of the Inner Mammal Institute and author of *Habits of a Happy Brain: Retrain Your Brain to Boost Your Serotonin, Dopamine, Oxytocin & Endorphin Levels*.

Kenna Griffin is a mass communications expert on the faculty of Oklahoma City University.

Rick Hanson is a psychologist, Senior Fellow of the Greater Good Science Center at the University of California, Berkeley, and the author of *Hardwiring Happiness: The New Brain Science of Contentment, Calm, and Confidence*.

Marlu Harris is a relationship coach and psychotherapist.

Celeste Headlee is an award-winning journalist and the host of the Georgia Public Broadcasting program *On Second Thought*.

Sophie Janicke is a positive-media psychologist on the faculty of Chapman University.

Homaira Kabir is a women's leadership coach and cognitive behavioral therapist.

Stacey Kennelly is a writer with the Greater Good Science Center at the University of California, Berkeley.

Scott Barry Kaufman is scientific director of the Imagination Institute at the University of Pennsylvania's Positive Psychology Center, and coauthor of *Wired to Create: Unraveling the Mysteries of the Creative Mind*.

Brian Knutson researches the neural basis of emotional experience and expression and is a professor of psychology and neuroscience at Stanford University.

Jaime Kulaga is on the faculty of Ashford University. She is a mental-health expert, life coach, and the author of *The SuperWoman's Guide to Super Fulfillment: Step-by-Step Strategies to Create Work-Life Balance*.

Nathaniel Lambert is a social psychology expert, formerly with Florida State University.

Robert L. Leahy is a cognitive therapy expert and the author of *The Worry Cure: Seven Steps to Stop Worry from Stopping You*.

Bruce Levin is a psychiatrist and psychoanalyst.

Daniel J. Levitin is James McGill Professor Emeritus of Neuroscience and Music at McGill University and the author of *The Organized Mind: Thinking Straight in the Age of Information Overload*.

Sonja Lyubomirsky is on the faculty of the University of California, Riverside, and the author of *The How of Happiness: A New Approach to Getting the Life You Want*.

Jane McGonigal is a game designer and author of *SuperBetter: The Power of Living Gamefully*.

Kelly McGonigal is a health psychologist and lecturer at Stanford University and the author of *The Willpower Instinct: How Self-Control Works, Why It Matters, and What You Can Do to Get More of It*.

Michelle McQuaid is a positive psychology expert and coach and coauthor of *Your Strengths Blueprint: How to Be Engaged, Energized, and Happy at Work*.

Caroline Myss is a renowned speaker in the field of human consciousness and the author of *Invisible Acts of Power: Channeling Grace in Your Everyday Life*.

Kristin Neff is a self-compassion expert on the faculty of The University of Texas at Austin and the author of *Self-Compassion: The Power of Being Kind to Yourself*.

Shasta Nelson is a speaker and founder of GirlFriendCircles. She is the author of *Friendships Don't Just Happen!: The Guide to Creating a Meaningful Circle of Girlfriends*.

Susan Nolen-Hoeksema was an American professor of psychology at Yale University and the author of *Women Who Think Too Much: How to Break Free of Over-Thinking and Reclaim Your Life*.

Michael Norton is the Harold M. Brierley Professor of Business Administration at Harvard Business School and coauthor of *Happy Money: The Science of Happier Spending*.

Doug Oman is a researcher in spirituality and health on the faculty of the University of California, Berkeley.

Caren Osten is a writer, journalist, and positive-psychology life coach.

Paul Piff is a researcher and expert on social hierarchy on the faculty of the University of California, Irvine.

Robert C. Pozen is on the faculty at MIT Sloan School of Management and the author of *Extreme Productivity: Boost Your Results, Reduce Your Hours*.

Emily Pronin is a perception-bias expert on the faculty of Princeton University.

LaRae Quy is a leadership coach and the author of *Mental Toughness for Women Leaders: 52 Tips to Recognize Your Greatest Strengths*. Previously she was an FBI counterintelligence agent.

Kirsten Sanford is a neurophysiologist and science communicator, also known as "Dr. Kiki." She is the founder of the program "This Week In Science" at KDVS-FM at the University of California, Davis.

Emma Seppälä is science director of the Center for Compassion and Altruism Research and Education at Stanford University and the author of *The Happiness Track: How to Apply the Science of happiness to Accelerate Your Success*.

Timothy Sharp is on the faculty of the School of Management at the University of Technology Sydney and the founder of the Happiness Institute.

Mary Spio is the founder of CEEK Virtual Reality and the author of *It's Not Rocket Science: 7 Game-Changing Traits for Uncommon Success*.

Kathryn Tristan is on the faculty of the Washington University School of Medicine and is the author of *Why Worry?: Stop Coping and Start Living*.

Marianne Williamson is a spiritual teacher and lecturer and the author of *Everyday Grace: Having Hope, Finding Forgiveness, and Making Miracles*.

ABOUT THE AUTHOR

Michaels Photography

As Director of *Forbes* WomensMedia and CEO of Positivity Daily (an inspiring career site for women), Nancy Clark has been working for more than 15 years to help women succeed and live happy, fulfilling lives and careers. Nancy loves to teach positive psychology-based skills and enjoys giving science-backed research in concise, fun examples. She also has a strong science background—her first job was in rocket science with NASA's Jet Propulsion Laboratory—and sees immense potential in techniques used in positive psychology.